SOMOS CHICANOS

SOMOS CHICANOS

Strangers in Our Own Land

by David F. Gomez

BEACON PRESS BOSTON

Beacon Press books are published under the auspices
of the Unitarian Universalist Association
First published as a Beacon Paperback in 1975
Simultaneous publication in Canada by Saunders of Toronto, Ltd.

Printed in the United States of America

9 8 7 6 5 4 3

Library of Congress Cataloging in Publication Data
Gomez, David F.
Somos Chicanos: Strangers in Our Own Land.
Includes bibliographic references.
1. Gomez, David F. 2. Mexican Americans.
I. Title
E184.M5G62 301.45′16′872073 73–4628
ISBN 0–8070–0510–X
ISBN 0–8070–0511–8 (pbk.)

DEDICO ESTE LIBRO

A

MIS QUERIDOS PADRES

Y

A LOS HIJOS

DE

RICARDO CHAVEZ-ORTIZ

Photo by John Taboada

Contents

"These children are also sons and daughters of God . . . think about the injustice that is being done to them." — Ricardo Chavez-Ortiz. Photo by David F. Gomez

Acknowledgments

In preparing this book, I was greatly helped and encouraged by several people who deserve special mention: Chicano writer Frank del Olmo of the *Los Angeles Times,* who read the entire manuscript as it was being written. Rocio Amezcua, a dear *Mexicana* friend in Mexico City, who helped with materials she gathered for me in the Mexican capital. Esteban Sanora helped me prepare the Epilogue. Joanne and Floyd McManus, also close friends, read the manuscript and offered valuable suggestions from an "Anglo" point of view. And Ray Bentley, my editor at Beacon Press.

I have relied on a great number of secondary sources, most of which are documented in the chapter notes. In writing Chapter Two, I relied on Carey McWilliams's *North from Mexico* (1948), which is still the best one-volume Chicano history book in existence; Leonard Pitt's *Decline of the Californios* (1966), the most scholarly and in-depth account of Chicanos during the last half of the nineteenth century; and Otis Singletary's *The Mexican War* (1960), an excellent, unbiased account of the conflict which raged between the two countries.

Photo by John Taboada

Vocabulario

Note: *Mexican American, Mexican,* and *Chicano* are often used interchangeably, although *Chicano* usually has a more militant or activist connotation to it. *Mexicano* always refers to a person who was born and reared in Mexico.

Many terms used by today's Chicanos would not be recognized or understood by Spanish-speaking peoples elsewhere; these terms are part of a patois or hybrid language (a mixture of Spanish and English) that originated in the *barrios* of the Southwest where young *pachucos* (see below) coined their own vocabulary.

Most of the Spanish or *pachuco* words and phrases have been translated within the text. The following are those that are not or that appear so frequently that it may be of use to list them:

Anglo — a white, non-Mexican American. Sometimes refers to all non-Mexican Americans, whatever their skin color.

Arroyito — small stream or creek.

Aztecs — Indians who established a highly advanced civilization in Mexico (ca. 1200–1520).

Aztlán — the Chicano nation. Literally, "white land" in Nahuatl (Aztec language). Historically, this "white land" was the ancient northern kingdom (probably today's Southwestern United States) of the Aztec tribes before they migrated south to what is today Mexico City. Chicanos claim the Southwest as their ancestral heritage and domain because of their ancient blood ties with the Aztecs and also because the land was forcefully and unlawfully taken from their nineteenth century Mexican forebears.

Barrio — Chicano neighborhood or community; literally, "district."

Bracero — Mexican field hand, or one who works with his arms (from *brazo,* arm).

Campesino — field worker; literally, one from the "fields" *(Campos).*

Cantina — Mexican tavern.

Carnalas — (*pachuco* orig.) sisters.

Carnales — (*pachuco* orig.) brothers.

Carnalismo — (*pachuco* orig.) roughly, the quality of fellowship, brotherhood, et cetera.

Chicano — poor Mexican American or *Mexicano* living in the United States. Definitely pejorative, the term is of disputed origin. One theory is that the Mexican Indians pronounced "Mexicano" as "Meh-chee-cano" and then shortened it to "Chicano." It is now popularly used by Mexican Americans who are conscious of being part of a people who are proud of their ethnic and racial identity, history, et cetera.

Compadres — godparents.

Conquistadores — conquerors; the sixteenth century Spaniards who defeated the Aztec warriors in battle.

Ejido — communal land of a Mexican pueblo (village).

Enganchado — someone who has been hoodwinked, deceived, or "hooked."

Ese — (*pachuco* orig.) hello, hey.

Gabacho — (*pachuco* orig.) Anglo (derogatory).

Gachupin — Spaniard (derogatory).

Gringo — Anglo (derogatory).

Hacienda — large, sprawling ranch or farm.

La Raza — literally, the "Race" or "People." It refers to all Mexicans north and south of the border; or sometimes, as *raza,* to all Spanish-speaking people of color (*gente de bronze,* bronze-skinned peoples).

La Raza Cosmica — the Cosmic Race or People, a term coined by nineteenth century *Mexicano* philosopher José Vasconcelos. According to his concept, *mestizos* would form the cosmic, ideal race because they are a racial mixture of New World Indians and Mediterranean-European stock, and tropical climates have historically nurtured higher civilizations than temperate ones. This concept was the Mexican response to racist Anglo-Nordic historians who rejected Mexican people as inferior, semi-civilized "half-breeds."

La Raza Unida Party (LRUP) — literally, the "United People or Race" Party. It is a third party movement in American politics inspired and sustained by Chicanos who seek to establish political self-determination for *La Raza*. Founded by José Angel Gutiérrez, the party is working toward complete political control by Chicanos in areas where they are the majority of voters, or to organize Chicanos into a "swing vote" where they are a substantial minority of voters. LRUP began as a reaction to the broken promises and hypocrisy of the Democratic party.

Machismo — Mexican masculinity, which according to some misguided Anglo commentators is a national and cultural trait and ideal of Mexicans everywhere.

Macho — Mexican male obsessed with demonstrating his sexual potency (stereotype); Mexican he-man; literally, "he-mule."

Malinche — Indian princess who fell in love with Cortez and helped him in the conquest of her own people; any *vendido* ("sellout").

Mariachis — Mexican musicians who play traditional Mexican music with guitars, violins, trumpets. The musicians wear the distinctive *charro* (horseman) garb of boots, tight-fitting pants, bolero jacket trimmed with silver ornaments, and *sombrero* (wide-brimmed hat).

Mayate — (*pachuco* orig.) a black American.

Mecha — acronym for *Mexicano Estudiantil Chicanos de Aztlán*, a Chicano movement group on college and university campuses. *Mecha* is the *pachuco* word for match (to light a fire). *Mechistas*, students who belong to

Mecha, subscribe to the *Plan Espiritual de Aztlán* (see below) and are supposed to work both on and off campus toward establishing *Aztlán* as a reality in their communities.

Mestizaje — race mixture, miscegenation.

Mestizo — person of mixed blood; a Mexican.

Mexicano-español — Mexican-Spaniard; one born of *conquistadores* and Indian women and who participated in the last stages of the conquest of Mexico as well as the exploration and settlement of the borderlands (Southwestern United States).

Migra — U.S. Border Patrol.

Pachuco — *barrio* tough or gang member; the term is of unknown origin. It usually refers to Chicano youths of the 1930s and 40s who wore outlandish clothes (zoot suits), spoke a language all their own (*pachuco* or *caló*) and belonged to *barrio* gangs. They were a "rebel" generation that defied the attitudes, dress, language, and conventions of the dominant society of which they were a part by birth but which they sensed had long rejected them and their people. In turn, general society justified the *pachucos*' judgment by prejudging them as violence-prone criminals and later making them the targets of racially inspired violence (zoot-suit riots).

Patrón — work boss.

Pelado — common man.

Placa — the individual name or *barrio* identity of a Chicano or Chicano gang written in distinctive Chicano script (usually on exterior walls and sidewalks).

Plan Espiritual de Aztlán — the "spiritual blueprint of Aztlán" was a declaration of Chicano independence drafted by young Chicanos at the Denver Youth Conference in April 1969. It states in part that "the Chicano inhabitants and civilizers of the northern land of Aztlán from whence came our forefathers, reclaiming the land of their birth and consecrating the determination of our people of the sun, declare that the call of our blood is our power, our responsibility and our inevitable destiny."

Poblador — settler.

Rico — rich landowner in the Mexican Southwest.

Rucos — (*pachuco* orig.) old men.

Vaquero — literally, "cowboy," from *vaca,* cow.

Vato — (*pachuco* orig.) guy, fellow from the streets.

Vato Loco — (*pachuco* orig.) "street crazy," Chicano in the *barrio* with "nothing to lose but his hostility" toward an unfair, unresponsive system or society; some writers refer to the *vato loco* as the modern-day *pachuco* or, like the *pachuco*, another example of the Chicano Existential Man. The *locos* are young, their ages usually range anywhere between twelve and twenty-one.

Photo by John Taboada

Introduction

THE AIM OF THIS BOOK is to share with readers, both Chicanos and Anglos,* what it means for me and millions like me to be part of a great people, *La Raza*, a nation within a nation. My story—as well as the history of *La Raza* in this country—shows that it is a tragic, painful, yet beautiful thing to be Chicano.

Many of us have lived within two mutually exclusive worlds. Which one do I choose? The process by which I am able to affirm the best of both worlds is not only what I or others must personally undergo, but what *La Raza* has been undergoing on a collective basis. Individually and together, Chicanos have been deeply engaged in the struggle to be free of all that prevents us from being fully human, fully Chicano, fully citizens of this country.

For generations we have been strangers in our own land. This inferior or second-class status has been imposed on us by military conquest, discrimination, and exploitation. Despite the fact that we have been colonized and treated as a conquered people, we have always affirmed that Chicano is beautiful, and we have struggled against the forces oppressing us. Today that struggle has escalated and is being fought all across this land, because the Chicano movement has brought more of us together than ever before. It is also the struggle of all oppressed, alienated peoples.

In this book I have tried honestly and candidly to share my own experiences and personal quest for identity as a Chicano by beginning with a brief autobiographical sketch.

*"Anglo" in this context refers to all non-Chicanos.

Hopefully, it will illustrate the growing consciousness and feelings among Chicanos everywhere. It is out of such a consciousness that today's Chicano is questioning, challenging, and confronting white society's values, beliefs, and institutions.

The succeeding chapters briefly trace the origin, background, and present-day conflicts and joys of *La Raza* in the Southwest. We have our leaders and heroes: César Chavez, Corky Gonzales, Reies Tijerina, José Angel Gutierrez, Ricardo Chavez-Ortiz. . . . We also face formidable, almost impossible odds, because we are and always have been a captive nation within an oppressor nation that has continually attempted to destroy our soul and spirit. We have been kept poor, ignorant, politically impotent, and subservient, but we have kept our dignity and pride and sense of injustice.

What are our goals and expectations? Assimilation for some of us with lighter skin color would be the easy way out. But it would let our hearts be cut out and thrown into the "melting pot" for which the oppressor nation is notorious. I do not believe assimilation is worth the price of my soul. And many Chicanos think as I do. We want more than absorption into an already decadent culture. We know who we are, we are proud of it, and we don't want to lose this sense of identity. Chicano wisdom, intelligence, muscle, and creativity built this nation—which was (in the Southwest) once our own. Perhaps one day we all may be able to share the land with its riches, prosperity, and opportunity. But not under the present system. For the terms of sharing must be *mutually* liberating.

Not everyone, of course, will agree with this book's interpretation and analysis. That is to be expected. In this regard, it is significant that in 1932 the entire Los Angeles community, including several prominent Mexican American businessmen, repudiated the work of muralist David Alfaro Siqueiros because of its social protest theme. In political exile from his native Mexico, Siqueiros was commissioned to paint a decorative mural on the exterior wall in the old plaza of Los Angeles. When the finished work was unveiled, a work the artist dedicated to the Chicano people, viewers were shocked and angered to find that he had painted a naked man—a Chicano—crucified on a double-cross with the American eagle, a symbol of the American dollar, proudly perched over the cross. The artist was expelled from this country because of his subversive views and the mural covered with whitewash.*

The "subversive" view of this book is that Chicanos are still being crucified in this country. While it is a message increasingly heard by Chicanos and Anglos alike, there are still those who may try, in whatever ways available to them, to minimize or whitewash that fact out of existence.

But the Chicano movement has brought too many of us together, and we have become too strong to be completely silenced or dismissed.

*See "Viva Siqueiros," in the *barrio* magazine *Con Safos* (No. 7, Winter 1971), pp. 26–27.

(Above) Chicano vato loco. *His plastic earring contains a small picture of Our Lady of Fatima, who is revered by Roman Catholics as the Virgin Mother of God. Photo by Carlos C. Garcia*

(Right) Photo by John Taboada

Chicano talking with his girl. Photo by Carlos C. Garcia

Chicano Easy-Rider in East L. A. Photo by David F. Gomez

"We are Mexicans; we live with the cockroaches and in the most unworthy conditions one could imagine in this land." — Ricardo Chavez-Ortiz. Photo by Carlos C. Garcia

"Placas" *(names of* barrios, *gangs, and individuals) are distinctively painted in Chicano script on the wall above. True Chicano graffiti, as an artistic form, is entirely free of profanity and expresses one's personal, communal, and geographical identity. It is also an attempt to express dominion and control over an environment which has all too often been abused and exploited by "outsiders." Photo by Carlos C. Garcia*

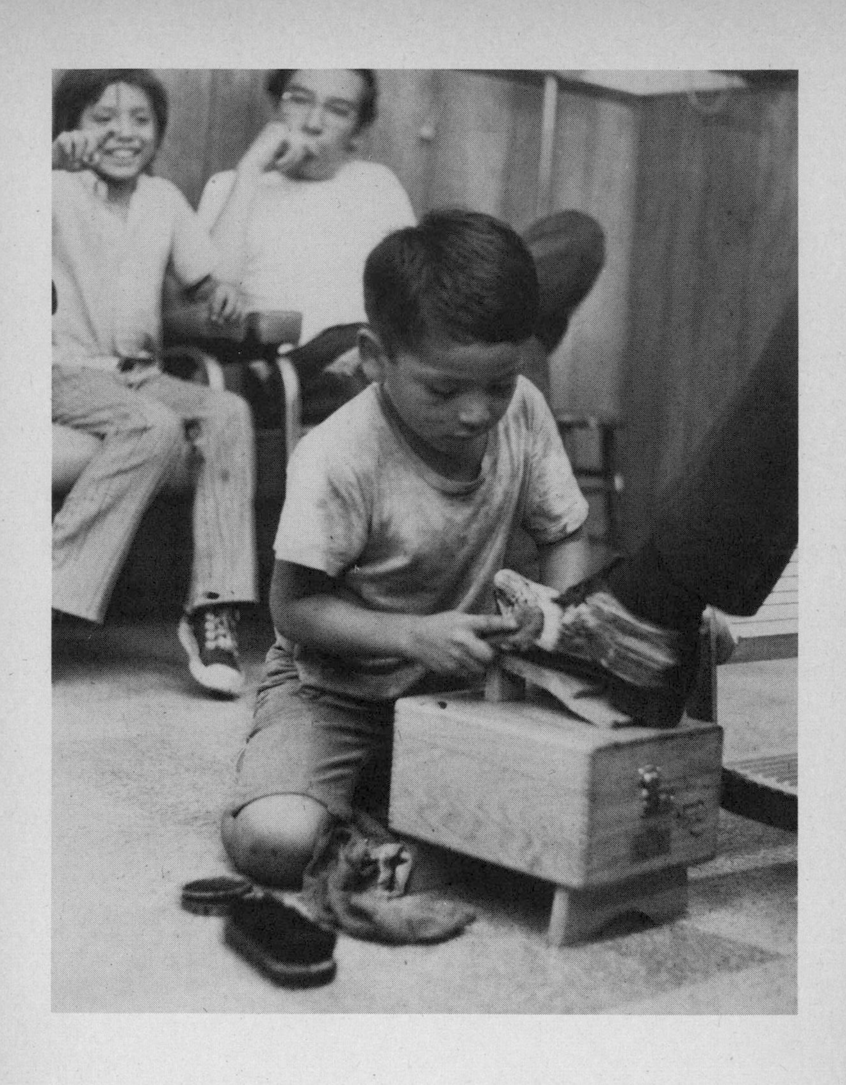

Eddie, a five-year-old "bolero" *(shoeshine boy), told us he was trying to make some money shining shoes to take home to his mother and family. Photo by Carlos C. Garcia*

Half of all Chicano children drop out of school before the twelfth grade. But it is the racist schools that have failed, not the children. Photo by David F. Gomez

Saturday afternoon along Whittier Boulevard. Note the merchandise displayed on stands and clothesracks along the sidewalk, according to Mexican custom. This cultural reinforcement attracts customers but is no more than a lure because barrio *stores charge higher prices and credit rates in exchange for inferior goods. Photo by David F. Gomez*

Small grocery store along East First Street in East Los Angeles. Most barrio *grocery stores, too, charge higher prices than stores outside Mexican or minority areas. Photo by David F. Gomez*

Two Chicanitos from the Maravilla projects in East L. A. What kind of future are we preparing for them? Only time will tell. Photo by David F. Gomez

August 29, 1970 — "a date vividly inscribed in the memory of every Mexican in the Southwest." The date marked the killing of Ruben Salazar, Chicano newsman, by a sheriff's deputy in East L. A. The officer was not reprimanded or brought to trial. The "CLF" to the right of the two Chicanas stands for the militant Chicano Liberation Front. Photo by David F. Gomez

View from the barrio. The maguey *plant (left foreground) is a familiar sight in the Mexican Southwest. In the distance, the Los Angeles skyline can be seen. Photo by Carlos C. Garcia*

Chicanos demonstrate for justice, human decency, and respect. Sign on the far left says, "We demand justice and an end to racist laws."
Photo by Carlos C. Garcia

FRONTIER

(Top) "Good afternoon. This is your friend Ricardo-Chavez-Ortiz." Wearing the captain's hat and wielding a .22-caliber pistol, Chavez-Ortiz begins to speak over a live radio hookup from the plane, protesting the treatment of Chicanos in the United States. Photo by Octavio Gomez, KMEX–TV News

(Bottom) Frontier Airlines 737 Jet sits on the runway at Los Angeles International Airport. Inside, Ricardo Chavez-Ortiz held his press conference. Photo by Octavio Gomez, KMEX–TV News

Central portion of David Alfaro Siqueiros' mural in the old plaza of Los Angeles. Over forty years have passed since the mural was white-washed; the outlines of the crucified Chicano and the American eagle perched on top of the double-cross can be clearly seen. Photo by David F. Gomez

CHAPTER ONE

Yo Soy Chicano

I

—Perdimos todo—decían mis padres
Cuando me platicaban de la revolución
No era que teníamos tanto, pero allá todo se quedó.
. . .
Yo siendo niño e inocente también
No entendí de lo que me hablaban
Por que viéndoles allí, cerca de mí
Yo nada había perdido.

—OCTAVIO IGNACIO ROMANO-V.[1]

("We lost everything," said my parents
when they spoke to me of the revolution.
"Not that we had very much but we left it all behind."
. . .
Being only a child and innocent of such things
I didn't understand what they said,
Because seeing them there, close to me,
I had lost nothing.)

BOTH MY PARENTS came from northern Mexico to the United States while they were in their early teens. Mamá came from Culiacán in the state of Sinaloa, and Papá came from the state of Sonora. They came with their parents, leaving everything behind except a few personal belongings and hope for a better life in the north. With millions of other Mexicans, they came in the wake of a violent revolution at home. They did not leave Mexico because they wanted to but only because the land was too poor to support them, and it was said that there would be better-paying jobs and a better life in the United States.

Papá never said much about life in Mexico, perhaps because we children showed so little interest. But occasionally, when the family gathered together, he would tell us about the farm in Sonora where he grew up. Living on the farm was always hard, but it became impossible after some soldiers from Pancho Villa's army stole my grandfather's livestock. The soldiers said they were not stealing, only borrowing the mules to feed the hungry troops. Actually, they were lucky not to be "borrowed" along with the mules to do service in Villa's Division of the North, but my grandfather was too old and my father too young.

Papá sometimes spoke with regret at having left Mexico because there were fewer opportunities for him in the United States. When he arrived, he had to learn a new language, adjust to another way of life, and end his formal schooling, which had begun in Mexico, in order to help support the family. "I didn't want to leave Mexico and I asked my father to leave me behind, but he wouldn't hear any backtalk. *'Nos vamos'* (We're going!) he said, and of course his word was final. I cried all the way on the train. Who knows, maybe I could have made something of myself if I'd stayed in Mexico." The rest of us would argue with Papá, trying to convince him that to us he was the most important person in the world. But he would only shake his head, unconvinced by our words. During the Great Depression, Papá returned to Mexico in search of work only to find that conditions there were even worse than in the United States. He came back to settle permanently, but his sense of being uprooted remained as strong as ever.

The family settled in Southwest Los Angeles, then a predominantly white area. There were no blacks in the area, and only a handful of Mexicans lived there. In Los Angeles, housing discrimination is not so blatant as it is in other areas of the Southwest United States. If the Mexicans had a small family, enough money to buy or rent one of the neighborhood's lower-middle-class homes, and didn't mind living away from the *barrio,* they could easily get into many white areas without a major exodus of whites occurring. If the Mexicans were light-skinned and had non-Indian features it would be even easier to move there because the white residents could rationalize that the newcomers were "Spanish." I always considered my parents very handsome, perhaps because I used the same standard most white people used. They did not look like the "Gordo" comic strip stereotypes—short, fat, and dark.

My mother and father learned to speak English without any accent. They were proud of this achievement and passed it along to us. My sister and I in early childhood learned to prattle and baby-talk in Spanish, but once we started in school mostly English was spoken to us, although my parents always spoke to each other in Spanish. (Perhaps they sensed that we wouldn't "make it" in the outside world or even be able to learn in the classroom unless we spoke only English.) Besides having an unaccented facility with English we always had most of the lower-middle-class comforts of life. We lived in a comfortable house with a yard of our own. The backyard was very beautiful because my *abuelo* (grandfather), Don Doroteo Gomez, had planted and cared for a lovely rose garden as well as several fruit trees which regularly produced an abundant supply of fresh lemons, plums, apricots, figs, limes, and avocados. My *abuelo* knew how to take care of a garden from long years of experience as a farmer in Sonora, Mexico.

Don Doroteo was a true *Mexicano* patriarch who stood nearly six feet tall. His resolute face was distinguished by a handsome Zapata mustache and complemented by wise and sympathetic eyes—eyes which looked as if they had seen much in life and knew its true significance. According to relatives, he served for a time as a *juez* (judge) on a Yaqui Indian reservation in Sonora. Sometimes late at night, my father recalled, strange men would come to the door of their house looking for Don Doroteo to report serious crimes like murder which had been committed by the Yaquis. He would investigate the matter and fill out the necessary papers. Don Doroteo lived in this country for seventeen years, yet never became a citizen or learned the English language. It may have been that he planned to return to Mexico or may have considered his new home as a kind of extension of Mexico, surrounded as he was by his children, a large Spanish-speaking population, and a terrain and climate similar to that of northern Mexico. Unfortunately I was never to meet my *abuelo* because he died in late summer of 1940, three months before I was born. I grew up with only my parents' memory and an old photograph to remind me of him.

Papá had only a few years in school before he began to work full-time in the old Peerless laundry on Main and Slauson in Los Angeles. His family needed the money so he went to work. After he and my mother were married, Papá learned the trade of garment-cutter and earned a living, along with thousands of other Mexican workers, in the Los Angeles garment industry. Some writers have stated that Mexican parents don't encourage their children to get an education, but I clearly remember my father telling me, "Get a good education so you won't have to be a laborer like me." While my parents had some ambition for me, they never pushed me to succeed at school. Nor did they keep after me about being a high achiever in school. Occasionally they asked me to keep up with homework assignments, but they never checked up on me.

What they did teach me most effectively and what I learned best from them was that they loved me no matter how well or poorly I did in school or anywhere else. The most important thing in life was not excelling in school but being a good and loving person, taking care of your own people, and living a life of dignity and respect. I belonged to a *familia* that accepted and loved me because of who I was, not for what I did.

II

Through brown eyes, seeing only brown colors and feeling only
brown feelings . . . I saw . . . I felt . . . I hated . . . I cried . . . I tried.
. . .
While, on the side . . . I realized I BELIEVED in
white as pretty,
my being governor,
blonde blue eyed baby Jesus,
cokes and hamburgers,
equality for all regardless of race, creed, or color,
Mr. Williams, our banker.
I had to!
That was all I had.
Beans and Communism were bad.

—JOSE ANGEL GUTIERREZ[2]

MY EARLY SCHOOLING was a terribly destructive experience, for it stripped away my identity as a *Mexicano* and alienated me from my own people, including my parents. At the age of six I entered Seventy-fifth Street School, which was located down the street we lived on. The school was predominantly white, at least 85 percent or more. The rest of us were either Mexican, black, or Oriental, but mostly Mexican. The teachers in the school were white, and for the next twelve years I never encountered a nonwhite teacher in the system. In the classroom my most vivid memories are those of Dick, Jane, and Spot in the first- and second-grade readers. Dick and Jane, of course, were white children, and even their dog Spot looked white and clean. Everything that was of value or importance in school was white and clean. The teachers either ignored our Mexican heritage completely or referred to us condescendingly as "Spanish." At first it annoyed me to be called Spanish because Papá had strictly taught us to say, *"Soy puro Mexicano"* ("I am 100 percent Mexican!") when asked what we were. The white teachers obviously knew what we were but, filled with good intentions, probably wanted to soften the ugly sound of "Mexican" by calling us Spanish. On the playground, of course, it was a different matter. The white children called us "dirty Mexicans" (that's why our skin was brown) or cowards who ran from fights (like our ancestors at the Alamo). My predominant impression, therefore, was that Mexicans had no legitimate place in the white world. If we Mexicans wanted to survive at all, we would have to become white. And I wanted to be white.

My mother came to visit me only once in school. It was during my year in the third grade. Mamá said that after school let out she would take me shopping with her. I expected to find her waiting in the car out front as she usually did when she picked me up, but instead she parked the car and came into the building to get me. By the time she got upstairs to the classroom it was 2:00 P.M. and the last bell had rung. Most of the other children were putting away their books and papers, getting their coats and sweaters from the cloakroom, or huddling around the teacher's desk. Everyone seemed to be talking very loud or laughing—as only children can do when the school day has ended. My mother entered the classroom through the front door, and when she saw me she called out, *"Davíd, apúrate, te 'stoy esperando!"* I froze with embarrassment and shame, feeling that everyone in the room was staring at us. And I didn't want the other children to think of me as different or foreign. I ran up to my mother and pleaded, "Mother, speak *English* please!" She never mentioned the incident, but I know I must have disappointed her.

My parents kept close contact with the land of their birth. It is about 140 miles from Los Angeles to Tijuana, and about 200 miles to Mexicali. Many of my relatives would head south across the border to have dental or medical work done. They went not only because the work could be done less expensively but also because they would be better able to communicate with the doctor in their own language. My parents did not have any language problems, but we would head south anyway just for the recreation and the opportunity to visit with friends and relatives there. My brother's *padrinos* (godparents) lived there, and that was a special relationship that linked our families closely together. Each summer my sister and I would swim in the *arroyito* with local Mexican children and enjoy ourselves, but later it seemed that we enjoyed ourselves just as much at home. Besides I didn't like the steady diet of beans and tortillas that our hosts served with every meal. Back home we had beans and tortillas with supper only, but in Agua Caliente we had it with every meal.

Gradually I became aware of feeling that what my family had to offer—language, customs, food, ways of looking at the world, vacations in Baja California—was not very good in comparison with the other world in which I lived. This was the world of little Richard Yates, Donald Cook, Patricia Allen, and the other white kids who went to Seventy-fifth Street School with me. I went out of my way as much as possible to get into their world.

My early childhood playmates, other than my own relatives, were white children, and I preferred their companionship to that of my own people. There was one little boy (whose name I've since forgotten) who was in the third grade with me. I wanted him to be my friend because he seemed to embody all that I admired and believed was best. He had blond hair, bright blue eyes, and rosy cheeks. In fact, he looked a lot like Dick, the little *gringo* hero in our first- and second-grade readers. And I was determined to make friends with him. On the playground during recess, I went up to him and offered him the supreme sacrifice I was capable of offering, my leather pouch, a valuable little pouch made of soft leather which I had saved box tops for months to finally get. You could wear the pouch on your belt and carry a lot of marbles or candy in it. "Here," I said to the little blond boy, holding up the pouch so he could take it, "do you want it?" "Yeah . . . don't you need it?" He seemed more puzzled than gratified by my generosity. I told him I didn't need it anymore and he could have it. So he took my pouch—but not my friendship—and went off to play in another corner of the playground with his own friends. Perhaps I somehow knew all along that I couldn't buy his friendship and that all I would succeed in doing would be to pay homage to the symbol of what I most admired and wanted to be.

Our principal at Seventy-fifth Street School was an elderly, soft-spoken lady with silver-white hair and an unctuous but dignified smile. At assemblies she led us through the flag-raising ritual, pledge of allegiance, and the morning prayer. Naturally, Miss Kelly impressed me as a very fine, religiously sensitive person. At least she did until the day I was called into her office. No one had told me what it was all about, and I was nervous as the secretary ushered me into Miss Kelly's office. It was a stern, almost severe office with a large reproduction of Gilbert Stuart's George Washington—the kind one sees in most public schools—hanging from the wall. She sat beneath the portrait and behind the largest desk I had ever seen. I stood there terrified by her presence but also curiously fascinated by how much Miss Kelly and George Washington looked alike. They even had the same phony smile.

But Miss Kelly wasn't smiling this time. "We know," she said in a deliberately harsh voice that quivered with indignation, "we know for a fact that you have been playing with a knife on the playground. And don't try to deny it because people have seen you!" I didn't try to deny anything because I was too scared and too numb to protest my innocence. I only knew that everything she was saying about me was completely untrue. So I stood there, knees shaking and completely defenseless before my judge and jury—condemned by Miss Kelly and George Washington! After pronouncing me guilty, she dismissed me with a final warning. "We don't want people like you playing with the other children. If I don't have that knife soon, I'm going to call your parents and have them come in." For a long time after, I was in a state of shock. How could anyone be so wrong about me? Days passed, and nothing happened. Later on, another student who heard it from someone else told me the whole thing had been a case of mistaken identity. Another Mexican boy named Michael Moreno had scared some of the small children with his pocket knife, and the principal had gotten the wrong Mexican—me.

Like many Mexican American children my school experiences made a peripheral person of me. My Anglo-white experiences at school so completely conflicted with my Mexican-brown experiences at home that I rejected one for the other only to find that I couldn't fully participate in either. I became a withdrawn person living on the periphery of the white world and wanting to have less and less to do with the brown world. And having been taught Mexican good manners at home I waited to be invited into the white world which I saw as all-important and superior to my brown world. But no one in the white world would invite me in. I should have realized that the Anglo-white promise of acceptance and equality was a total lie and a double-cross, but still I held out hope. So I waited and waited, and gradually waiting became a way of existence—existing in neither the white world nor the brown. I was indeed a "Mexican American," a hyphenated person who was somehow both Mexican and American yet neither a Mexican nor an American in any clearly defined sense.

Sometimes when the brown world intruded into the white, I felt divided within myself, but usually I ended up choosing the white world. Most of the time, I was simply a displaced person who, in his better moments, should have realized he was trying to be someone or something he actually was not. I believed that I was white, a belief that left permanent scars on my consciousness because it uprooted me from my *familia* and created in me the false and deceptive impression that I was really accepted and belonged in the white world. All the while I believed or wanted to believe I could be accepted by whites, the real way in which white society perceived me was being permanently carved into my personality. I wasn't an equal but only a weak and inferior being. (Close friends have confided to me that the first impression I gave them was one of *weakness*. The way I spoke to them and looked made them think I was weak. Only after getting to know me were they able to see that despite this appearance, I was not like that at all.) I give many people the impression of being weak because I have been a marginal, peripheral person in a dominant society for so long that unconsciously I assumed all the characteristics that the dominant group expected of me.

Being a *Mexicano* in Anglo-land caused me the most frustration and pain during junior and senior high school. When I entered John Muir Junior High I began to take an active interest in girls, which was natural enough for a thirteen-year-old boy. But the only feminine beauty I had been conditioned to see was white. Rosalind Russell, Jean Simmons, and Doris Day were my movie favorites. What I saw on television or in magazine pictures only reinforced my conviction that the only beautiful women or girls were white. I found myself staring at and wanting to touch *gringitas.* There were also many Mexican girls in school, but if they did not look like *gringas* I didn't feel they were attractive. The white standard of beauty affected my little cousin María in an especially tragic way. She was in grammar school at this time, and I remember her as being small for her age with large, dark eyes, long, shiny black hair, and a very swarthy complexion. Years later, María bitterly recalled her childhood and how her mother often powdered her face to make the little girl look less like a dark *Mexicana* and more white. Thus she would be more acceptable to white society and, by obvious implication, to her mother as well. To most Mexicans, swarthiness is a sign of beauty, but to many of us who were caught up in the values of the dominant society, it was only a badge of inferiority. For that reason I should have realized that the little *gringas* were as far beyond my reach as the movie stars I gaped at. The very standard that made them so attractive to me also made me ultimately unacceptable to them.

At school I played alongside tough Mexican boys from the *barrios.* They wore their clothes in *pachuco* style, wearing their Levis and khaki trousers low with unbuttoned sport shirts outside the trousers. They combed their hair in a ducktail (a style they had originated) and wore dark sunglasses both indoors and outside—even if the sun was not out. They were *vatos locos,* always fighting with the *mayates* or *gringos* or, if no one else was around, they would fight among themselves. They were as tough as young men come; and as a sign of how mean they were they wore small cross-shaped tattoos on the backs of their hands where the thumb and index finger meet. Their *placas* (names of *barrios* or gangs) were distinctively drawn in Chicano script on sidewalks, school walls, or any wall or surface they could reach with an aerosol spray can or magic marker without being caught by the police. One of the *vatos,* Ricardo, tried to befriend me. He had noticed how I dressed and spoke (more like the *gringos* I was imitating than a Chicano) and approached me between classes to ask me about it. "Hey, *ese,* aren't you a Mexican? You don't talk like one. . . ." "Yes, I'm a Mexican," I answered defensively, trying to avert his look. He was only trying to be a friend in setting me straight, but from then on I avoided him whenever I could.

Later there were times when I looked back and wished that I'd become one of the *locos.* At first I thought they were unashamed to be Mexicans, unashamed to proudly assert the very differences the rest of us sought to deny, conceal, or powder over. But I now realize that I had more in common with the *vatos locos* than I knew at the time. We were actually in the same situation. No longer Mexicans and denied the full status of white Americans, we were only doing our best to be somebody. We were trying to define our identities as best we knew how. The *vatos* wrote their names on walls and made obscene gestures at The Establishment as if to say they knew who they were and didn't need anyone else. On the other hand, I was trying to crash the gates of *gringo*-land, believing that I would be who I wanted to be once I got in.

When I entered John C. Fremont High my best friend was Leo Garcia. He was a big Chicano, standing about six feet tall with a handsome face and very dark coloring. I owe a great deal to Leo, for he did what the school had been unwilling and unable to do. Leo convinced me that I had the ability to succeed in my studies and persuaded me to take college preparatory courses in high school. Leo had a good mind and saw the importance of learning. He would astound everyone by reciting from memory the batting averages and other lifetime statistics of Babe Ruth, Ty Cobb, and other baseball greats. He took me under his wing, and I developed a real interest in reading and doing well in class. I had planned to take a trade school course like auto mechanics, which all the Chicanos and blacks had been counseled to take. But Leo convinced me that it would be better to prepare for college and the better jobs available to college graduates. The courses were harder than I expected, but gradually I improved. Besides, I was so well-behaved and stood in such contrast with the troublesome *vatos* and blacks that my teachers rewarded me with good grades.

During our high school days Leo and I had several run-ins with the law. As far as I could tell the only reason the Los Angeles Police Department had for picking us up so often was that we were Mexicans and to them Mexicans were more likely to be *marijuanitos* (dope addicts) than anyone else. The first time it happened was the most memorable, perhaps because it was the first. On a Saturday evening in the fall of our freshman year, Leo and I were walking home after playing baseball in the park. We had played hard all afternoon until it was so dark we couldn't see the ball anymore. As we walked along Vermont Avenue, not far from Slauson, Leo carried most of the playing equipment in a canvas athletic bag while I carried the bat over my shoulder. From out of nowhere an unmarked police car pulled alongside of us and came to a halt. Two plainclothes detectives got out of the car and ordered us to drop what we had in our hands and roll up our shirt sleeves. When they didn't find any needle marks they started questioning me about the "menacing" way I'd been "brandishing" the bat. Leo didn't like the rough treatment and antagonized them by answering their questions in the same belligerent tone of voice in which they were being asked. In response the police put us both in the patrol car and took us to the local station. They took Leo into a separate room and tried to break his spirit by browbeating him for at least an hour, but he didn't give in. Meanwhile, they had decided that I was a *good* Mexican because I had not talked back to them or questioned their authority (actually I was scared speechless). But they called Leo "stupid" because he didn't know how to "keep his big mouth shut." Then they let us go because we had not done anything. That was the first of many such experiences.

Although the police may not have thought so, Leo and I were very much alike. We were equally attracted to the other world which good grades and high school honors promised us. By the time I graduated from high school I had applied to and been accepted by Loyola University in Los Angeles, and Leo was planning to attend Los Angeles City College. My first day at Loyola was a frightening experience. This was not due merely to my having to travel to an unfamiliar part of town for the first time or face the totally different world of the college campus by myself. I was terrified because never before had I seen so many white people of college and adult age all together at the same time. In high school my classmates were either Chicanos or blacks, and the last time I had been in a predominantly white school was my last year in junior high school. At Loyola, I felt like a foreigner in a strange land. One of the things that struck me so forcefully at the time was that the white fellows, most of whom were seventeen or eighteen years old, looked as if they had to shave every morning, something many Chicanos and blacks like myself found unnecessary. It made me feel like a mere boy among grown men.

That first afternoon at Loyola, I found that the feeling of alienation was not just a product of my imagination. Those same people who so terrified me by their whiteness and made me feel out of place actually considered me an alien. In order to register for courses we had to sign up for them with individual registrars who checked our registration materials and made sure we were eligible to take the course. All freshmen were required to take a foreign language, and I chose Spanish. I got into the line for the Spanish courses, but when my turn came and I gave the registrar my registration cards, she looked at the name on the cards and then looked at me and exclaimed, "You can't take your own language!" She strongly suggested that I should concentrate on mastering English first. I was so overcome with confusion that I simply turned away and went to the back of another line. That semester I ended up taking beginner's French.

In my first year of college I wanted to be a part of the white world so badly that I did something I regretted for a long time after. I enlisted in the Marine Corps Officer Training Program. Of all things, a recruiting poster in front of a post office attracted me. It pictured a Nordic-looking, strong, and independent *Macho*. If being a Marine had done that for him maybe it could do the same for me—or so I thought. Like so many Chicanos who join the Marines, I was prompted to join up because of my sense of *machismo*. After all, our only image of manliness was what we saw on television and in the movies: John Wayne fighting for America's freedom at Iwo Jima or the Alamo. But for me there was more: I believed that by becoming a Marine officer I would at last find acceptance. If only I could wear the Marine uniform people would forget what I wanted to forget more than anything else: my dark skin, coarse black hair, and Spanish surname. It didn't work out that way because after six weeks of summer training I couldn't pass the written tests and was flunked out of the program. My heart wasn't in the program, and in that sense my failure was a fitting end to something I should never have attempted to be: a white *Macho* whom other whites would accept and admire.

I never told my parents about my failure because I didn't want them to be ashamed of me. While they naturally would have been disappointed, they would have shown me the same *cariño* I had always experienced within the *familia*. But the world of Anglo values which stressed success and frowned on failure dominated my actions. I was cut off from my parents in a more profound way than just the generation gap. I was also cut off from my Mexican roots. Nor was I able to look to Leo for friendship or emotional support. He had dropped out of college after the second year, and that, coupled with his being a Mexican (a mirror image of the identity I had tried to put behind me) led me to have less and less to do with him until we were no longer friends. Leo was the only Chicano I knew who had gotten as far as college with me (a remarkable achievement for Chicanos!), and it seemed almost natural for him, as a Chicano with his roots still in the *familia,* to drop out. He was also the last Chicano I would have as a real friend for many years to come. At least in the way I treated Leo, I had indeed become the *gabacho* I so desperately wanted to be.

Another factor, far more significant, was that I wanted to be a priest, and Leo no longer had any place in my life. Loyola University, an all-white Catholic men's school run by the Jesuits, was a perfect place to nurture this vocation. During my three years as a student, no one took an interest in me socially. No fraternity ever approached me. No school organization went out of its way to invite me to its social functions, such as dances with neighboring girls' colleges. In place of a social life, I joined the Sodality, a religious organization on campus, went to daily Mass, and read the lives of the saints. When I left to enter the seminary I did not think anyone was concerned about me. After three years, I did not have a single friend on campus to say goodbye to. Almost ten years later, when Father Charles Casassa retired as Loyola's president, his farewell advice to the students and faculty was a plea for them to be more outgoing and welcoming to minority students, especially the Mexican Americans on campus. The advice came ten years too late to do me any good.

The example of my parents had much to do with the nurturing of a vocation to the priesthood. In many ways they were typical Mexican Catholics. They always made sure that we children attended our catechism lessons and received our first communion and confirmation. My mother kept blessed religious statues around the house. In her bedroom was a statue of the Sacred Heart encased in glass with a votive candle burning in front of it. A statue of St. Martin de Porres was displayed in another room. Very popular among Mexican people, St. Martin was a seventeenth century Dominican lay brother who was barred from the priesthood because he was a mulatto; yet he went on to become one of the most popular saints in the Spanish-speaking world (perhaps because most Spanish-speaking people with mixed blood could sympathize and identify with him). My father's deep faith expressed itself in many ways. The good deeds and favors he did for our neighbors and relatives profoundly impressed me. He is the kindest, most generous man I have ever known.

After deciding to enter the seminary, I applied to the Paulist Fathers for admission, and later that summer, after taking all the required verbal and written psychological tests, I was accepted. Paulists work mainly with white Americans in the major cities of the United States, and it was this image that first attracted me to them. For instance, I recall being impressed by a vocation pamphlet which happened to be given to me. On one of the illustrated pages there was a picture of a Paulist Father preaching from the pulpit of a large church. The caption read: "Imagine yourself preaching in the great cathedrals of America!" The people in the congregations of the "great cathedrals of America" were all white, and I was influenced by this. The needs of the Mexican people never entered my mind; they did not exist for me. I wanted to work among white people and to get as far away as possible from Mexicans (and in the process I was to get far away from myself). My intention was not that deliberate or explicit in my consciousness, but my unstated presumption was that anything important in either spiritual or temporal matters was happening among white people alone.

The Paulist seminary in Washington, D.C., like seminaries everywhere, resembles a forbidding castle surrounded by acres and acres of open land. Such institutions were deliberately planned that way because seminaries are literally supposed to be "seed beds" where young vocations are carefully planted, nurtured, and protected from the outside world, especially from contact with women. The system was designed to produce men who would faithfully carry on the centuries-old tradition of a celibate clerical way of life and ministry, and the system worked very well. For nearly eight years of priestly training I kept my needs and feelings well suppressed and underdeveloped and within the logic of celibate, clerical spirituality, it all made good sense.

The priesthood, among other approaches I tried, was a way of "crashing the gate" and having an identity to be proud of. With such an identity I didn't have to be my real self, and only after ordination as a priest would I come to be more in touch with my real self and recognize my need for close relationships and intimacy. My need was for someone to say, "I love you for yourself; I like being with you because you're you." I was fortunate enough to have one or two friends in the seminary who wanted to assume that relationship as close friends, but I was not ready for it then. Instead I took cover behind the imposed identity of "Father Gomez." This identity was, unlike that of most professions, all-embracing. I was Father Gomez from the moment I awoke in the morning to the time I went to sleep at night. This self-imposed role as well as that imposed by other people's expectations enabled me to hide from the responsibility of friendship or any mature love relationship which, in turn, hindered my overall self-awareness.

During the six years of my seminary training, I was the only Mexican American in the entire student body. The vast majority of seminarians were Irish-Americans from the East Coast. (A year before I entered, there had been a black seminarian from Virginia who had lasted only a year at St. Paul's. In my opinion, he was expelled from the seminary for racist reasons. The Paulist faculty had voted to oust him—or so I heard from other seminarians—because he could not "preach very well," i.e., his Southern black accent was something white congregations could not be asked to tolerate.) I got along pretty well with most of the other seminarians although some of them had a hard time figuring out what I was. Some thought I was Chinese at first, or an American Indian. Others asked me if I was a light-skinned black. I'd answer that I was a Mexican American and try to change the subject. Talk about race and nationality still made me uncomfortable. Most of the seminarians didn't even bother to ask which doesn't surprise me now. How could these Easterners be expected to know or be curious about Mexicans when they did not even know what a Puerto Rican was, and many of them had come from cities with large Puerto Rican *barrios?*

Once a seminarian asked me if I'd ever experienced discrimination, and, thinking that that meant being turned away from lunch counters or barber shops, I responded, "No, I never have." In fact, I resented the question because it singled me out as being a member of a nonwhite minority. On another occasion a seminarian whom I disliked (and who obviously disliked me) called me a "half-breed." When I heard that word I froze; it was as if someone had recognized me and was naming me for the first time since I'd left L.A. The shame and anger I felt made me want to kill him, but seminary life had so strongly reinforced my timid, quiet nature that I let it pass.

My seminary training was, for the most part, a valuable and enriching experience. My old-fashioned spirituality was updated, and my love for Christ was deepened. The Second Vatican Council had finished its work in Rome as I began to study theology. Like most seminarians at the time, I looked upon myself as a crusader for renewal, and, armed with the teaching of the Council Fathers and the Scripture, we would renew the Church. It was an exciting time to be alive and preparing for the priesthood.

My training reshaped my approach to Christianity. It was no longer rosary beads and prayer books and churches but a *life* to be lived to the full. Our basic approach was Christ-centered, and because Christ was fully human the way to develop a truly Christian outlook was to take man seriously. This brand of man-centered Christianity was expressed by the German theologian Dietrich Bonhoeffer: "To be a Christian does not mean to be religious in a particular way, to cultivate some particular form of asceticism (as a sinner, a penitent, or a saint) but to be a man. It is not some religious act which makes a Christian what he is, but participation in the suffering of God in the life of the world."[3]

My man-centered theology was also expressed in a story Martin Buber, the Jewish philosopher, was fond of quoting: "Each day of Atonement the rabbi of a small community would quietly slip away from his synagogue and be gone for a few hours. One of the rabbi's disciples suspected that he might be meeting secretly with the Almighty and followed him to find out. The disciple only saw the rabbi put on the coarse working clothes of a peasant and go to the cottage of an invalid widow, where he cleaned her house, prepared her food, and ministered to her in her illness. The disciple, when he returned to the synagogue, was asked, 'Did the rabbi ascend to heaven?' He reflected for a moment and answered: 'If not higher.'"[4]

Besides studying theology and philosophy, extracurricular projects such as census-taking in local Washington parishes also took up some of my time. One year some of my fellow seminarians invited me to join them in their work in Sacred Heart parish in Northwest Washington, a parish with a large concentration of Spanish-speaking people: Cubans, Puerto Ricans, Mexicans, and other Latin Americans. It is significant that I became interested in serving the Spanish-speaking because of white seminarians who had learned the language on their own initiative and, again on their own initiative, had become pastorally involved in a Spanish-speaking parish. Despite my earlier ideas, despite my "white" thinking, I was beginning to learn about the needs of my own people.

III

But now . . .
I've been told that I am dangerous.
That is because I am good at not being a Mexican.
That is because I know now that I have been cheated.
That is because I hate circumstances and love choices.

—JOSE ANGEL GUTIERREZ[5]

Ordination was a critical turning point because it freed me from the unreality of the seminary and put me on my own in a parish assignment. There I discovered the seminary had prepared me to be a good Catholic priest but not necessarily a good human being. My duties were to preach, teach, offer Mass, and be an official spokesman for the Church. But these duties, which I faithfully discharged, were aimed at preserving the status quo and not rocking the boat. The Church, with its racism, apathetic constituency, and autocratic leadership, was basically conservative and unchanging. Even when the Second Vatican Council inspired an unprecedented wave of activism and social concern (along with a preoccupation for being "relevant") among priests and nuns, the institutional Church was still incapable of dealing with the problems of people in society. It occurred to me that the Church as an institution—the Church of cardinals, bishops, priests, and nuns—was far better at taking up collections for church buildings and property than working for the liberation of the poor and oppressed. I don't remember when I stopped thinking like a Catholic priest and became a Chicano. It was a long and complicated process, but maybe it began in Utah, where I was first assigned to work.

Each year in early April when the rest of the country is crowning Cherry Blossom queens and enjoying springtime, a well-seasoned, highly mobile army of poor people sets out on the thankless and almost impossible mission of harvesting this nation's crops. Thousands of Mexican migrant workers—

men, women, and children—leave South Texas in search of field work throughout the United States. They are a strong and courageous little army, able to travel vast distances without rest and spend long hours under the blistering sun at backbreaking stoop labor. When they leave home, families of ten or twelve crowd into cars or pickup trucks and travel for fifteen or twenty hours straight, stopping only for gas. Many travel as far as Michigan, North Dakota, and Washington State. At harvest time there is usually enough field work for the entire family, but the labor contractor's promises of good wages* and decent living conditions are never kept. The year I was assigned to work in a parish in northern Utah, several hundred migrant families were brought into the area to harvest sugar beets, cucumbers, and cherries.

Many of the families had no choice but to settle in the dilapidated shacks and huts located in the ruins of an abandoned sugar refinery. Inside the shacks there was no running water, and outside there was only a single shower unit for 200 people. The toilet facilities were crumbling wooden outhouses which most of the people were afraid to use. The migrant camp was hidden from view of the main road, and it took me a long time to find it. At first I hesitated to visit the new tenants because I didn't know if I could be of any real service to them. As it turned out, they were of great service to me by welcoming me and making me feel at home. We liked each other from the start, and several families accepted me as one of their own.

That summer I met regularly with the children, offering them remedial education classes in the camp. One weekday evening was set aside for the teenagers. We formed a Teen Club which provided the only social life they had, apart from their families. Manuela Valdez, an attractive eighteen-year-old girl, became my best student and helped me organize activities. She impressed me as being more mature and responsible than the others. Manuela not only put in a full day's

*Annual income for a migrant family of four is $1,400.

work in the fields but also took care of six younger brothers and sisters in the camp. She was born in Mexico, had attended school there, and spoke such excellent Spanish that it was a pleasure to listen to her conversation. Most of the other children over twelve worked all day in the fields with their parents and were always tired in the evenings when we met.

Signs of fatigue showed more on Manuela than the others. When she began to miss more and more meetings, I went to the shack where they lived to find out what was wrong. Mrs. Valdez told me not to worry, that Manuela was just overworked and that extra rest would make her better. Toward the middle of Summer, the migrants packed up their few belongings and moved on to Oregon and Washington in search of more crops to harvest. By October most of them had returned to Texas after six months in the migrant stream. A few months after their return, Manuela died from an acute and fatal form of anemia.

When the news eventually reached me, I felt like burning down the migrant camp and getting a gun to go after everyone responsible for the conditions there: The Utah and Idaho Sugar Company who owned the land the camp was on. The Mormon farmers who leased the land and allowed their hired workers to live in filth and squalor. The county health and welfare officials who did absolutely nothing to help my people. At about the same time several cases of iron-deficiency anemia and one fatal case of typhoid were discovered among the few migrant families that had remained in the area. Many of us brought these cases to the community's attention, and as a result county health and welfare departments were pressured into helping the migrants. In fact there was so much adverse publicity about living conditions that the entire camp area was fenced off and the shacks and huts completely razed. All our efforts, however, were at best stopgap measures. The field workers needed a union, something César Chavez was just then beginning to organize in Delano, California.

And in still another sense our efforts were futile. Manuela was dead, *y algo dentro de mi tambien se habia muerto.*

About this time I made a special trip to Denver to visit with Rudolfo "Corky" Gonzales of the *Crusade for Justice.* Through friends I contacted Emilio Dominguez, one of the Crusade's leaders, who put me up in his own home and introduced me to Corky. I had read about the Crusade's efforts in Denver as well as the Youth Conference that had been held a few months earlier; out of that conference the *Plan Espiritual de Aztlán* had been formulated, and MECHA had been born. Corky generously spent time with me, answering my many questions about the Chicano movement. I came to see that the movement was not limited to Utah or Colorado but was happening wherever Chicanos took pride in themselves and their *raza;* it was not limited to the cause of the migrant workers (which then was getting the most publicity) but had been rooted in the cities for generations and was now being "rediscovered" by Anglos and Chicanos alike. And as we parted, Corky gave me a copy of his poem, "I am Joaquin," and it reinforced more than anything else I'd read my own growing awareness and feeling of solidarity with him and with our entire *raza.*

Another important development for me at this time was falling in love with a girl from San Francisco. We met briefly that summer, and at first our relationship was kept up by letters. Then it grew to be more personal and intimate. The following summer I visited her, and the relationship grew even more involved for us. I was visiting her every chance I got. This caused a tremendous crisis in my life because I was hopelessly caught between two conflicting loyalties and commitments: the priesthood and her. But I was afraid to make the choice—it seemed too risky. The Church said I was doing wrong, and the Church was, in a sense, my mother who had given me everything I valued most dearly. But the Church did not own me; in my conscience and heart I believed I was doing the right thing and that in this instance the Church was wrong and to obey would be self-betrayal.

Prayerfully and thoughtfully I weighed the alternatives and consequences for months, and it was in this context that I came to the conclusion that what I enjoyed with her—our mutual relationship of love, trust, and confidence—was best for me as a man and as a Christian. I was prepared to make the awful sacrifice of leaving the priesthood and the Paulists for her. I had to be my own man. She had been able to reach behind the identity I had assumed, making me confront myself and everything my life as a priest stood for; and at the time I thought she gave more meaning to my life than anything else. As a priest I had talked and preached about love, but until I was actually in a love relationship with her I could not experience or know the meaning of love. She may not have realized it at the time, but she made a man of me that year. Never before had I been happier or more in control of my life and destiny on that personal level. A life and destiny I was prepared to fully share with her.

It was the first time I had gotten that close physically and emotionally to a white woman (was that the reason I found her so attractive?) or any woman for that matter, and it taught me a lot about myself and others. The truest freedom for me, I discovered, was being bound in love to another. But such freedom frightened her even more than it had me; she could not accept what I was willing to share with her—myself. When she turned away, more controlled by her fears than her love, I became terribly angry, more enraged than ever before in my life. And my anger slowly turned to sadness, disappointment, and torment. In that moment of intense and painful emotion, I discovered that she needed me more than I needed her because I would recover my losses and love again (having learned from the experience), but she was afraid to love and, in that sense, I discovered that I was the stronger person. It was a sensation of strength I had never before experienced.

The following year proved to be even more of a challenge to me and gave me further insight into my strengths, which I had been unaware of until then. Two of my classmates assigned to the Paulist Center in Boston knew that I was on the verge of leaving the active ministry and invited me to join them in their ministry and thus give the priesthood another try. I flew to Boston from the West Coast and talked with them about the decision I was trying to reach. They listened sympathetically and then made me the most beautiful offer I've ever received: they wanted me to join them with no strings attached to my staying or leaving. They wanted me to be my best self even if that meant leaving a week or a month after I arrived. What mattered most was my happiness.

In Boston, we formed a team ministry and worked as closely as possible alongside the people, as ministers and not as "leaders" or "religious superiors" over them. Most of the people we attracted and worked with had been ex-Catholics, people who had been alienated by the official Church but had found something religiously meaningful in the experimental liturgical and social action center we established. During this time, I became more critically aware of the Church as an institution and how badly it had abused so many people in the past. Through reflection, I was able to distinguish clearly between the Church as an *institution* like all the other institutions in society, and the Church as a *people,* full of belief, love, and hope. As a people, the Church was beautiful and alive; as an institution, it was outmoded, clergy-dominated, and in need of radical reform (all conclusions of the Second Vatican Council which local church leaders refused really to accept or act on).

My year in Boston was extremely valuable for it gave me time to think about my life, my vocational problems, the Church, the needs which I experienced and had for so long denied. My work in the social action center we established was made challenging and satisfying when I discovered that thousands of Spanish-speaking people live in the Boston area. It was estimated that there were forty thousand Puerto Rican people alone. We launched an education-recreation program for Puerto Rican children living in Boston's South End. And I felt the same sense of solidarity with the children and their parents as I had with my migrant friends from Texas.

During the year I fell in and out of love again, which

helped convince me that there was something missing, that I couldn't be honest with myself and those whom I served while continuing to live as a representative of the institutional Church. The decisive factors were the personal love and intimacy which I had shared with those whom I allowed myself to love and who loved me, and the faith which my classmates had placed in me. Today, my classmates remain my closest friends. The events of the previous two years caused me no small amount of confusion, frustration, and fear. And for a long time, I was deeply troubled and dominated by a sense of failure—a sense that I had failed my own people by not staying within the institution to help reform it and make it responsive to them. But I realized that it had to be; I couldn't stay within the institution and continue to be myself, my best self.

Despite my sense of failure, or perhaps because of it, I became more aware of my strengths; more aware of the identity I had been born with and which I had rejected from the moment I had been brainwashed and conditioned by Anglo society into thinking and believing that white is good and brown and black are bad. Taking stock of my life—my ability to suffer, fail at things I attempted, be vulnerable again despite my losses and defeats—I concluded that I am more than my failures. What I am as a Chicano and as a man is something to be proud of. And without this pride I would be lost; I would be without anything of permanent and lasting value. For the first time I found myself in a position to accept myself without illusions of someone else's identity, without any pretenses whatever. It was at the age of thirty, then, that I decided to start again at the beginning, without any other identity than the one I share with my brothers: *Yo soy Chicano.* I am just a man.

My parents always taught me to be proud of who and what I am. "Be proud of what you are!" my father would shout at me. It was almost as if he was aware of what was happening to me and was trying to drown out what society had been doing ever since I started school. With his roots closer to Mexican soil and the Mexican spirit, he never lost pride in who and what he was. But the same pride in our *raza* was nearly eradicated from my being. I had to try, fail, and be completely lost and abandoned, in order to find myself. White society very nearly achieved its stated end and purpose by *gringo*izing me and throwing my heart into the melting pot. But not quite. Today I admit that I am not white, and that I do not want to be white. I am a Chicano. To make such an admission is for me to rip away the mask that I have assumed for too long.

Perhaps the ancient pride of my fathers has been redeemed in me. I hope so.

NOTES

1. Octavio Ignacio Romano-V., "Yo no Perdí Nada," *El Grito* (Vol. IV, No. 2, Winter 1971), p. 66. My translation follows the original text.

2. José Angel Gutiérrez, "22 Miles," *El Grito* (Vol. I, No. 3, Spring 1968), p. 40.

3. Dietrich Bonhoeffer, *Letters and Papers from Prison* (New York: The Macmillan Company, 1953), p. 233.

4. Aubrey Hode, *Martin Buber: An Intimate Portrait* (New York: Viking, 1971).

5. José Angel Gutiérrez, *op. cit.*, p. 41.

CHAPTER TWO

Who Are the Mexican American People?

WHO are the Mexican American people?

That may be an impossible question to answer because we are so highly diverse and even unpredictable. We are peace-loving and friendly, yet we started the first bloody revolution in the twentieth century. Vindictive and unforgiving, yet for three centuries we patiently worked on our own land as peons for the *gachupin patrón* who had taken it from us in conquest. Fiercely emotional and hot-blooded, yet intellectual enough to chart the heavens with startling accuracy and build magnificent pyramids whose sheer geometrical precision was our way of praising the gods of the Sun and Moon. José Vasconcelos called us a cosmic people whose racial identity spanned an ocean and enshrined the best of two worlds. *La Raza Cosmica!* A race that would inherit the earth.

But many of us are far from agreeing on a common identity. We use many names to describe ourselves: Hispano, Latino, Mexicano, Chicano, Mexican American (with or without the hyphen!). Perhaps as Abelardo, the Chicano poet, has hinted, *La Raza* is best because it is a word which not only means "people" but "plain" or "bottom." We are, after all, *gente raza*—plain, unnoticed, often forgotten people who have been at the bottom of society for generations. Perhaps we were destined to inherit the earth in the gospel sense—as the poor, oppressed, and crucified.

Throughout our history, we have suffered and experienced every form of human bondage and destruction. Our country, our women, our sense of nationhood have been raped by the invading armies of foreign powers. In Mexico, the stinging curse and plaintive lament is one and the same: *¡Viva Mexico, hijos de la Chingada!* Long live Mexico, sons of the Violated One! Every form of violation and destruction. But never defeat. And because we have endured and survived, we reflect, above the misery and degradation, the grandeur, nobility, and strength of common people who refused to die or be conquered.

I

El 13 de agosto de 1521
heroicamente defendido por Cuahtémoc
cayó Tlaltelolco en poder de Hernán Cortés
No fue victoria ni derrota
fue el doloroso nacimiento del pueblo mestizo
que es el Mexico de hoy

(On August 13, 1521, the city of Tlaltelolco, despite a heroic defense by Cuahtémoc, was taken by Hernando Cortez. It was neither a victory nor a defeat but the sorrowful birth of the *mestizo* people who are the Mexican nation of today.)

—INSCRIPTION FROM A MONUMENT AT THE PLAZA DE LAS TRES CULTURAS, MEXICO CITY

IN TLALTELOLCO, which is today part of one of the world's most sophisticated cities, there is a unique monument of contrasts—*La Plaza de las Tres Culturas.* A spacious modern plaza surrounds the original cathedral church of Mexico, a church which the Spaniards forced their Indian captives to build immediately after the fall of Tlaltelolco. It must have been a heart-breaking as well as back-breaking labor because it was built directly over the ruins of an Aztec temple which the Spaniards had razed when they took possession of the city. Before the advent of the white man and his religion, the Indians had worshiped their gods in such temples. Near the stone church are the unearthed ruins of another Aztec structure, a pyramid, which the Spaniards had only incompletely destroyed. In the background but dominating the entire scene are large, ultramodern skyscrapers designed by Mexico's internationally famous architects.

The inscribed monument in the plaza is significant not only because it commemorates the victory of the Spaniards over the Aztecs—a victory which placed Mexico under Spanish rule for the next three centuries; but also because it makes the surprisingly honest (and for some, *painful*) admission that the event also marked the birth of the Mexican people, a *mestizo* people. What is surprising about the statement is that it could not have been made in Mexico during the first three hundred years of Mexico's existence; the race-conscious Spaniards would never have allowed it. In this sense, such an admission illustrates a growing sense of identity which has been taking shape since the time of Mexican independence in the last century. Only until recently, many Mexicans in the United States openly repudiated their Indian blood as though it were a sign of inferiority. This attitude among Mexican Americans is, of course, a reflection of Anglo-American racism but it is also rooted in the attitudes and institutions that the Spaniards imposed on the Indians and *mestizos* after the conquest.

Although the Spaniards intermarried with the Indians and allowed them to be baptized as Roman Catholics—which gave them a place, if only the lowest, in Spanish society—Indians and all other nonwhites were considered as inferior people by the ruling Spanish classes. Society was structured to place whites in positions of power and authority while mixed-bloods and Indians were ranked at the very bottom. Mexicans lived under this rigidly structured racial hierarchy until 1810, when the people rose up against their masters. It is no accident that the rallying cry for the revolution was "*¡Indepen-*

dencia! ¡Que mueran los gachupines!" (Death to the white Spanish devils!). Mexicans are no strangers to racial prejudice. They have lived and suffered under it ever since they were born as a people. It is a yoke they unwillingly bore and constantly sought to cast off.[1]

From the European's point of view, it all began in 1519 when Hernando Cortez landed at Vera Cruz on the coast of Mexico with 550 men, 16 horses, and a few cannon.

The Aztecs were betrayed from the beginning. Malinche, the Indian maiden of noble lineage, aided in the conquest by serving as Cortez's interpreter, guide, and mistress. She knew the Indian dialects, local legends, and superstitions. The Aztecs also had their neighboring Indian tribes against them; the Tlaxcalans and various other tribes in and around the Aztec capital became Cortez's allies out of jealousy and a desire to see their Aztec masters defeated and conquered. Also, the Aztec emperor Moctezuma believed he had been forsaken by his gods. Years prior to the white man's coming, signs and prophecies had pointed to the Aztecs' downfall at the hands of a superior force. Moctezuma felt completely helpless and orphaned at these signs because the white man was seen as a god whose time had come and whose coming meant the terrible end of their protector-gods.[2] Among the portents were the destruction of two temples by fire, a comet seen in the sky by day, and a woman's voice crying in the night, "My children, we are lost."[3]

Moctezuma's children were indeed lost as Tenochtitlan, capital of the Aztec empire, welcomed the white men. The emperor could have forcefully resisted their entrance but fatalistically accepted it along with his being taken prisoner. Cortez planned to subdue the populace and add the city to the empire of Spain, but Spanish greed and suspicion led to an incident which prolonged the conquest of Mexico and resulted in the loss of thousands of lives and the destruction of the entire city. During Cortez's absence from the city, his men brutally murdered two hundred Aztec nobles during a religious festival. In retaliation, the outraged Indian population turned on the conquerors and forced them to retreat to the imperial palace where Cortez, on his return, found them still besieged.

Moctezuma tried to persuade his people to stop the siege and allow the Spaniards to leave the city. Unlike their emperor, the Aztec warriors were not in a conciliatory or fatalistic mood. They stoned Moctezuma to death and continued with their efforts to defeat the Spaniards. With their principal hostage now dead, the Spaniards decided to retreat. On the night of June 30, 1520, Cortez and his troops attempted their escape by setting out across the causeways which enabled passage over the city's canals. They had not gone far when the alarm sounded. Less than half the Spaniards made it to safety outside the city. Many of them must have been a pitiable sight as they clutched their stolen treasures with one hand and tried to fend off hundreds of their attackers with the other. It had indeed been a *noche triste,* a sad night for the Spaniards as they were ousted from the city.

The Spaniards had to completely destroy Tenochtitlan and its defenders to reconquer it. Led by Cuahtémoc, a nephew and son-in-law of the murdered emperor, Aztec warriors would not surrender despite the knowledge that they would surely be defeated. According to Octavio Paz, the Aztecs believed their gods had willed defeat for them. Deserted by their Indian allies and former vassals, pitted against armored professional soldiers with superior military technique and weapons, abandoned by their gods, the Aztec warriors fought a life-and-death struggle they were destined to lose. Two months later, the city was reduced to burning rubble, and its defenders lay dead. Cuahtémoc was captured and hanged. But it would not be a Spanish victory in a later age; today there are no monuments in Mexico which honor Cortez, while Cuahtémoc is revered as a national hero.

When the white men first saw Tenochtitlan they exclaimed, "Are not the things we see a dream!"[4] What they so greatly admired was the product of a highly advanced civilization. The Aztecs were excellent architects, city planners, artists, craftsmen, statesmen, and warriors. Besides being builders, they were men of letters: poets, historians, philosophers, and theologians. Prior to the conquest they had created a loose federation of neighboring tribes who were on the verge of being absorbed into the Aztec empire. Had this been accomplished earlier, Cortez would have encountered even greater opposition; as it was, conflicting loyalties and jealousies among the different tribes worked to Cortez's advantage. The Aztecs, however, had accomplished a great deal in their efforts at empire-building. The Aztec language (Nahautl) was spoken from north central Mexico to Central America, and their civilization had been spread as far north as the Mississippi Valley, where Indians of the region developed Aztec-style religious and political institutions and constructed pyramid-like temples. Much more of their history could be known (for it was all written down) but for the book-burning, anti-pagan zeal of the Christian priests who presided at the destruction of entire libraries!

The Spaniards approached the task of colonization as they had the conquest: divide and conquer. Villages and towns were divided into *encomiendas,*[5] or royal tracts of land (including the Indians on the land), which were "entrusted" to a Spanish colonist *(encomendero).* Theoretically the Indians gave their commodity and labor tributes to the *encomendero* in return for military protection and cultural and religious education. But in reality the Indians were exploited, abused, and subjected to extreme deprivations. Besides paying regular tributes to their white masters, churchmen, local, state, and imperial officials, they were forced to support the friars and monks, build churches, monasteries, and roads, and work in the mines. The *encomienda* or "trust" belied an imperialistic and exploitative system which used raw power and force to get its way. Churchmen like Bartolomé de las Casas kept on insisting so often that the Indians were human beings, that the *Law of the Indies* was finally passed which stipulated that the natives should be treated like human beings. "But all the King's decrees, orders, and desires," wrote de las Casas, "will never hold back, as they have not to date, the incurable and insatiable greed and ambition of the Spaniards."[6]

It is a mistake to think that the Indian was completely conquered by the Spaniard. At the time of the conquest there were two kinds of Indian tribes. One was sedentary and agricultural; the other was wandering, isolated, and dependent on hunting and warfare for their living.[7] The first type was easily conquered within the first twenty-five years of Spanish occupation. They had no choice; they either submitted or were killed. They lived as a conquered people: heads bowed, despised, exploited, always fearful of the white man. The other group in the outlying regions never submitted to the Spaniard. There were Indian revolts and uprisings late into the nineteenth century. In 1825 the Yaquis began a campaign to exterminate the white man, and until 1850 the state governments of Coahuila and Chihuahua had to make treaties with the Comanches and Apaches. Like Cuahtémoc, these Indians never surrendered. The white man was always the *gachupin*—a liar, a thief, a rapist. To Tarahumara and Pueblo Indians, as Tannenbaum has observed, he was always lower than a pig.

Yet the face of Mexico today is a *mestizo* face. From the beginning, *mestizaje* took place at a rapid rate. The first generation of *mestizos* were claimed by their fathers and even took part in the last stages of the conquest. Later, *mestizos* helped with the exploration and colonization of other regions, including the Southwest. The reason that racist Spaniards so readily united themselves with native women was that native women were the only ones around. Later, when the first white women were sent to the Indies (usually they were slaves or prostitutes) the Spaniards preferred them in marriage over the native women. The Indian women were naturally sensitive to this, and one chronicler records that many Indian girls tried to bleach their skin to compete with their white rivals.[8] Even today Mexico has her own type of racial prejudice—Caucasian features and light skin are highly prized. But for the most part, it gradually evolved into one of caste and class discrimination rather than racial prejudice.

After four hundred years the Spaniard has vanished and

the Indian has prevailed. "The white man took all that he wanted—and he wanted all that he could take and absorb," wrote Frank Tannenbaum. "In the end he was himself taken in, he was himself absorbed."[9] Racial distinctions can no longer be made, and it is highly unlikely that there are really any "full-blooded" Indians left in Mexico.[10] They exist culturally, socially, and somatically, but all have been touched by the mixture of the races. For generations *mestizos* lived in a kind of limbo, belonging to neither the pure whites nor the pure Indians. They were looked down upon, regarded as socially and racially inferior, and denied full and equal opportunity. With the passing generations, Mexico would eventually become aware of her identity and even be proud of it. The large mural by Juan O'Gorman which decorates the exterior of the modern University of Mexico library is a splendid illustration of the Mexican racial and cultural identity. It depicts two human profiles merging into a full face. One profile is that of a Spaniard and the other is that of an Indian woman. The full face is that of the Mexican—the face of a *mestizo*. The fusion of the races favored the Indian; his blood and consciousness have survived and prevailed while the Spaniard was absorbed.

II

THE SOUTHWEST was first explored and colonized by Spanish, *mestizo,* and Indian pioneers. It is often assumed that white-skinned Spaniards undertook the burden of exploration and settlement and therefore should be credited with the achievement. But nothing could be further from the truth. It was largely a joint effort that involved all those who were brave enough to risk venturing into an unknown wilderness and strong enough to endure life on the desert frontier. Early expeditions into the region north from Mexico cost hundreds of lives. One survivor, Gaspar Nuñez Cabeza de Vaca, returned to Mexico City where he told incredible tales of his journeys into Arizona, Texas, and New Mexico. Francisco Coronado and an expedition of several hundred men followed in pursuit of the fabled Seven Cities of Cíbola and the Golden Quivera, a quest that would take them through Arizona, Texas, New Mexico, Colorado, and into Kansas. Other expeditions went in search of the northern region of Aztlan, where the Aztecs said they had first come from.

These explorations were for more kingdoms and empires to conquer and pillage, but the would-be *conquistadores* found only rugged mountains, scorching deserts, unending plains, rattlesnakes, and unfriendly Indians.[11] The Indians were considered savages by the newcomers, but these "savages" were shrewd enough to keep the gold-hungry *conquistadores* on a wild-goose chase for nonexistent kingdoms of gold for nearly a generation. *"Mas allá,"* the Indians said when asked about the fabled cities. "More over in that direction—(just don't stay here and do to us what you did to our brothers in Mexico)." But the stage had been set for a future settlement by men more inclined toward colonization than conquest.

Ultimately the Spanish plan for the region was to build a strong central colony in New Mexico and establish outposts in California, Arizona, and Texas, thus forming a line of defense enabling Spain to protect her borders and gradually integrate the region into the rest of the country. New Mexico was settled by Juan de Oñate and a large group of settlers in 1598. In 1609 Santa Fe was founded, making it the oldest state capital in the United States. Despite the violent revolt of the Pueblo Indians which ousted the settlers from the area, they returned and were to remain. In the late seventeenth century, Jesuit Eusebio Kino pioneered the settlement of Baja California and Arizona. At the beginning of the eighteenth century, Texas was settled in the areas of Nacogdoches and San Antonio, but settlement was extremely difficult despite the Spanish government's continuing investments of money and men. California was successfully settled around the time of the American revolution. Fray Junípero Serra and other Franciscan pioneers set up a series of twenty-one missions along the coast from San Diego to San Francisco, while four presidial towns (San Diego, Santa Barbara, Monterey, and San Francisco) and two pueblos (San Jose and Los Angeles) were established. The impressive achievement of colonizing the borderlands from Texas to California was accomplished by *Mexicanos-españoles,* a people who had synthesized two bloods—Spanish and Indian.

The Spanish-Indian-*mestizo* influence permeates every aspect of life and thought in the Southwest—in the economy, customs, laws, place names, speech, architecture, and institutions. When the first Anglo-Americans arrived in the area they found not a wilderness but a land settled and civilized by the people who had come north from Mexico. The real pioneers were to teach the Anglo newcomers about mining, sheep, cattle-raising, and irrigated farming. Mexicans had been mining silver and gold since the sixteenth century, and centuries later would teach the Forty-niners in California how to prospect for gold and instruct them in the main principles of mining law. And whatever the Anglos learned about mining silver and copper they learned from Mexicans whose skill, knowledge, and labor were in constant demand. The sheep and cattle industries in the Southwest were built on centuries of accumulated knowledge and labor of Mexicans whose Spanish fathers had brought the first sheep and cattle to the new world. The American sheepherder, cowboy (a carbon copy of the Mexican *vaquero* in every detail from his ten-gallon hat, *sombrero galoneado,* to his branding iron, Cortez having used the first branding iron in the Americas), and rancher contributed nothing original to the development of these industries in the Southwest. Irrigated farming was also a distinctively Spanish-Mexican-Indian contribution. The Moors taught the Spaniards how to irrigate arid land, and in turn the Spaniards brought this knowledge to Mexico where they learned even more from the Indians. The first irrigation systems in the Southwest were *Mexicano-español* in origin.[12]

The heritage of the Southwest is indeed a rich one. The Spanish-*mestizo*-Indian contribution also includes the names of states, cities, rivers, mountains, and plains. Besides cattle and sheep, the first pioneers brought goats, horses, pigs, cats, and barnyard fowl. They came with the first hoes, spades, plows, grinding stones, pliers, files, and wheels. They built *misiones, pueblos,* and *presidios* with adobe bricks and planted gardens, vineyards, and orchards. From their labors came the first harvests of pears, peaches, apples, plums, oranges, lemons, limes, cherries, grapes, figs, strawberries, raspberries, olives, dates, pomegranates, almonds, and walnuts. According to Carey McWilliams, Spanish-Mexican laws eventually were incorporated into Anglo law: the doctrine of water rights, the ganancial system of communal property rights for husband and wife, and the legal practice of granting leases allowing for the use of natural resources without giving the land outright to particular persons.

A lexicon could easily be compiled listing the Spanish words that Anglo-Americans use in their everyday speech. For example, alfalfa, alpaca, barbecue, barricade, canary, cargo, cigar, cannibal, canoe, chocolate, desperado, embargo, fandango, grandee, guerrilla, hurricane, indigo, maroon, mosquito, mulatto, mustang, maize, Negro, paragon, parasol, potato, quinine, sarsaparilla, sierra, siesta, sherry, soda, stampede, savanna, tobacco, tomato, tornado, vanilla.[13]

Anglo-Americans would later make their own invaluable contributions, but, when they arrived in the Southwest in the nineteenth century, they found a people waiting for them who had tamed a barren and forbidding wilderness. Millions of Mexicans living in the Southwest today are the descendants of those first pioneers.

III

> *Si el presidente de los Estados Unidos, Mr. Polk, puede demostrar que la primera sangre vertida lo fué en nuestro territorio, quedará justificado, pero si no puedo o no quiere hacerlo quedaré plenamente convencido que él fué quien ordenó al general Taylor que penetrara en un estado pacífico para provocar la guerra.**
>
> —A. LINCOLN, 1846 (*Inscription from a plaque in the War Museum, Chapultepec Castle, Mexico City*)

THE MEXICAN PEOPLE came into being as a *mestizo* nation in the sixteenth century as a result of Spain's desire for territorial conquest and military might which was superior to that of Mexico's Aztec defenders. Unwillingly, Mexico was made a colony of Spain, enslaved for nearly three hundred years. And less than forty years after the Spaniard was driven out of Mexico, the Mexican people were victimized by still another imperial conquest: this time by the powerful and expansion-minded giant to the north, the United States. The *Mexican American* people were to come into being not by choice or election but by the military force of the American government.

It is important to remember that, unlike other oppressed or marginal groups in this country, the Mexican along with the American Indian was conquered. The Indian was killed or driven off his land. Mexicans, however, were a numerical majority in their own land (except for Texas, where illegal American immigration was encouraged and supported by the United States) with a well-developed culture and autonomous government. When the Mexican could not be killed or completely driven off his land, he was colonized. The *gringo,* like the *gachupin* before him, was a *conquistador*.

> *¡Pobre Mexico! Tan lejos de Dios y tan cerca de los Estados Unidos.*
>
> —DICHO

> Poor Mexico! So far from God and so near to the United States.
>
> —PROVERB

*"If the President of the United States, Mr. Polk, can prove that the first blood spilled was on our own territory, he will be justified; but if he cannot prove it, or will not, I will be fully convinced that he was responsible for ordering General Taylor to invade a peaceful nation in order to provoke a war." The remarks enshrined in the Mexican capital are taken from Congressman Lincoln's speech in the U.S. House of Representatives, 1846.

During the early nineteenth century, most Americans believed in the doctrine of Manifest Destiny and were ready to occupy the entire continent to the Pacific Ocean—conquering everything and everyone in their path. Mexico had recently won her independence from Spain and was internally weakened by political and economic upheavals. Manifest Destiny influenced the purchase of Louisiana and brought the United States into a contiguous position with Mexico. As early as 1812, Luis de Onís, Spanish minister to Washington, reported to the viceroy in Mexico that he knew on good authority that the "ultimate ambition of the United States was to extend its boundaries to the Rio Bravo (Rio Grande) and to the Pacific."[14] This ambition would eventually lead the American government to provoke a war of aggression and imperialism against Mexico. In the meantime, the United States permitted its people to continue a steady flow of illegal immigration into Mexican territory. But Mexico was not strong enough to enforce her boundaries, and in 1819 the Adams-Onís Treaty stipulated that, in exchange for Florida, Americans would stay out of Texas.

White racism fanned the flames which led to all-out war between the two countries; it also rationalized subsequent injustices committed against Mexican American people. The prevailing American attitude toward Mexicans was revealed in the distorted and prejudiced accounts of life in the Southwest penned by several notable Americans, such as James Ohio Pattie, Thomas Jefferson Farnham, Richard Henry Dana, and Mary Austin Holley. They wrote highly judgmental reports of the Mexican people, their institutions, traditions, values, dress, education, politics, women; everything Mexican was held up to a severely critical and unfavorable light.[15] Some of these writers had no other basis for their thought than ignorance and bias; others wrote with the ulterior motive of rousing Americans to invade the Southwest or justifying the invasion of Texas that was taking place. In all cases they revealed the dominant American opinion that the Anglo-Saxon race was far superior to the Mexican race; that Mexicans were inferior because of their mixed blood ("a mongrel race"); and that the Mexican people would greatly profit from being conquered and controlled by racially and culturally superior Anglos.

"The half-breed as might be expected," wrote Farnham, "exhibits much of the Indian character; the dull suspicious countenance, the small twinkling piercing eyes, the laziness and filth of a free brute, using freedom as the mere means of animal enjoyment . . . their intelligence is quite limited."[16] And again: "No one acquainted with the indolent, mixed race of California will ever believe that they will populate, much less, for any length of time, govern the country."[17] Another Anglo critic wrote that the Mexicans of Texas are "very ignorant and degraded, and generally speaking timid and irresolute."[18] But if Mexicans were incapable of being free and responsible men, Anglos would improve their condition. "In the hands of enterprising people," wrote Dana, "what a country this might be!"[19] One Texas Anglo wrote: "The southern races must be renovated and a new vigor infused into them, and the United States are the *officina gentium* for the New Continent."[20] If ever a people truly deserved to be conquered it was, in the minds of Americans, the Mexican people of the Southwest.

The Mexican and American were bound to conflict in other ways as well. Americans were Protestants who had little or no tolerance for Roman Catholics; and the vast majority of Mexicans was Catholic. And many Anglos were native-born Americans who had an intense dislike for "foreigners" who spoke a different language from their own. There was a basic clash in value systems as well. Speaking generally, Mexicans were more oriented toward the present than the future. They enjoyed life day by day and believed that the end and object of work was leisure and pleasure (a view which has since been vindicated by those who repudiate the American "rat race"). Americans, on the other hand, were future-oriented and believed that hard work was synonymous with virtuous living. When the Anglos took over, there was no effort to integrate the good of one value system with the other. Mexican American values would be ignored or, in direct clashes, obliterated.[21] Americans who took pride in democratic institutions and ideals looked critically at the aristocratic society of the *ricos* with large land holdings in New Mexico and California. Yankees who desired land—from President Polk on down to the lowliest Yankee squatters and interlopers—were determined to take it from the Mexicans by any means necessary. When it came to taking land from Mexicans, the Yankees soon forgot their democratic ideals of due process and equal protection under the law.

The first United States thrust into Mexican territory was the Anglo invasion of Texas. Stephen Austin and other Americans were given permission by Mexico to settle in Texas. In turn they agreed to become Mexican citizens and Roman Catholics. But illegal Anglo immigration into Mexican territory mounted quickly, and by the 1830s the Yankees outnumbered the native Mexicans by at least five to one. There were innumerable Mexican abuses in governing Texas, and as a result open rebellion broke out but was soon crushed by Mexican troops. Future rebellions were to be more successful. It should be remembered, however, that both Mexicans and Yankees were united for a time under the Mexican-Texas flag (even at the Alamo) and were fighting for their own brand of *Mexican* independence and justice. Mexican fought against Mexican and suffered from the same abuses and atrocities by national troops. General Antonio Canales, for instance, led Texas troops against Mexican regulars until it became apparent to him that Anglos were fighting not for Texas independence under the Mexican flag but to bring Texas under United States control. Mexican historians would later conclude that the United States from the beginning intended to obtain the territory of Texas by any means necessary and to accomplish this end introduced her citizens into the area in ever-mounting numbers.[22] During the Texas revolt, Americans ". . . counted on effectual aid from the United States, which gave protection to them,—covert indeed but still decided and constant. Supplies for the war, arms, men . . . while [the United States] protested that it observed the most strict neutrality."[23]

The United States also had its eye on New Mexico and California. Several attempts had been made to purchase California, but the Mexican government refused to part with her strategically located borderland. The mission territory was rich and productive; fish and game were a constant lure to American fishermen and trappers. Captain John C. Fremont was dispatched to California to rouse the inhabitants into a Texas-style revolt, but because there was no provocation (as there had been in Texas) he was left with the abortive and embarrassing "Bear Flag" revolt. What saved face for Fremont (as well as his career) was that the United States declared war on Mexico at about the same time, so his disgraceful band of American trappers and adventurers—the so-called California revolutionaries—were legitimized and became the "California Battalion of Volunteers." Long before the United States had dispatched Fremont to stir up trouble in Mexican territory, American intentions were manifested in 1842 when Commodore Thomas ap Catesby Jones mistakenly believed that the United States had declared war on Mexico and landed at Monterey, where he captured the city and raised the American flag. A few days later when he found that no war existed, he quickly retreated with apologies to the native Californians. Incidents such as these served advance notice on the Mexican people that Americans wanted their land and were already preparing to seize it by force.

War came with the American annexation of Texas. The Mexican government withdrew its minister from Washington and refused to recognize the American claim to Mexico's colony. President James Polk dispatched troops under the command of General Zachary Taylor to the area between the Nueces and the Rio Grande allegedly in response to the Texas Republic's request for protection against possible Mexican efforts to reclaim her territory. When Mexico kept to her side of the border, American troops entered Mexican land and stationed themselves on the upper side of the Rio Grande. This led the Mexicans to start a defensive action against soldiers who clearly had invaded Mexican soil. The weak and ill-prepared Mexican army made a poor showing against American troops in northern Mexico but refused to surrender. As a result, the United States decided to bring Mexico to her knees by moving directly against her capital by way of Vera Cruz. When American troops landed on the Mexican coast, they followed the same route Cortez and his *conquistadores* had marched three centuries earlier.

By September 1847, General Winfield Scott and his invading army had fought their way into the Mexican heartland from Vera Cruz.[24] Scott's invading troops met the most heroic resistance not from seasoned Mexican regulars but from the boys at the *colegio militar*. The young cadets had stationed themselves at the Castle of Chapultepec and held their position against superior fire power for the better part of a day. When finally overpowered, they refused to surrender and, draped in Mexican flags, flung themselves from the castle's high walls to certain death below. Like their Aztec forebears who had defended Mexico three centuries before, the *niños heroes* had written some of the most glorious pages in Mexican history in their own blood.

The war against the New Mexico province was successfully executed by Colonel Stephen Kearney and his Army of the West (1,500 frontiersmen). In a brief campaign of only six weeks' duration, Kearney's army took possession of the area without major resistance from the people. Later the New Mexicans openly revolted against the invaders and killed Charles Bent, the American governor of occupation, but within two weeks all resistance was forcefully put down. The military conquest of California was effected by a joint army-navy-marine action. In the summer of 1848, the United States Navy moved against Monterey, San Francisco, and Los Angeles, quickly taking those key locations. A month later, however, the *Californios* had organized themselves and put up a strong resistance, even winning back Los Angeles. The native forces gained momentum and were soon in possession of most of the interior towns and were threatening the coastal gains of the Americans. In the Battle of San Pascual, Pio Pico and a troop of mounted *Californios* fighting only with lances of laurel, decisively defeated the Americans. But in the end they were overwhelmed by superior forces: a combined force of warships in the Pacific, marines, infantry, and cavalry. When Los Angeles was retaken, all formal resistance was broken, but the army of occupation had to quell several riots which broke out in the city protesting the foreign troops.[25]

IV

THE TREATY OF GUADALUPE-HIDALGO ended the war. Mexico had little choice but to sign; her capital was occupied by American troops, her provinces overrun by the enemy, and internally the Mexican government was torn asunder by political factions. Nicolas Trist had been delegated by Polk as diplomatic representative. He traveled with the American army so that negotiations could begin with the Mexicans whenever they could be brought to their knees and made to surrender. Polk had officially recalled Trist because the President had been severely criticized at home and felt that Mexico, not the conquering United States, should sue for peace. Trist received his orders to return to Washington at about the same time that the Mexicans were ready to negotiate a settlement. He decided on his own to proceed illegally because he felt that the opportunity for a settlement might not come again; the people in the capital were angry and on the verge of resuming hostilities rather than completely surrender to the Americans.[26]

On February 2, 1848, the Treaty of Guadalupe-Hidalgo was signed by the negotiators. The heart of the agreement is compressed into articles 5, 8, 9, and 10. Article 5 stipulated that the boundary between the two nations would be shifted so that half of Mexico (California, Arizona, New Mexico, Texas, Colorado, parts of Utah, and Nevada) would become

American territory. In return the United States agreed to pay Mexico fifteen million dollars. Articles 8 and 9 deal with the rights of Mexicans who would remain within the conquered lands. And article 10, which stipulated grants of land authorized up until 1846 by the Mexican government would be valid, was dropped by the United States at a later date.

The Mexican negotiators deserve much credit for the care and consideration which they gave to Mexicans left in the Southwest. One of them was alarmed that Trist (the only American negotiator) could demand California and New Mexico but completely overlook the rights of Mexicans, their land titles, and their religious rights as Catholics.[27] They also wanted to know whether or not Mexicans in the Southwest would remain citizens of their native land or become United States citizens. One negotiator lamented that unless their civil and religious and political rights were protected, they would become strangers in their own land.[28]

Articles 8 and 9, as summarized by Professor Feliciano Rivera, included these rights:

(1) Freedom from harassment that attempts to force Mexicans to give up their personal possessions—land, property, goods.

(2) Exemption from taxation resulting from the sale of property that can be traced to the original inhabitant.

(3) Protection under the United States Constitution and all subsequent legislation.

(4) Guaranteed equal treatment and equal protection under the law.

(5) Freedom of religion and religious property.

(6) Protection of culture which included language, clothing, music, food, and anything that could reasonably be construed as culture.

(7) Recognition of their land titles except as limited by protocol.

(8) Protection against state, municipal, or territorial ordinances that violate these rights.[29]

The treaty has never been honored by the United States. With the exception of freedom of religion, the guarantees have been flagrantly violated from the day the treaty was signed. Mexicans have been systematically and brutally deprived of their birthright. The treaty was actually a fitting testimony to the motives and ambitions of the United States—an illegal and unauthorized agreement which led only to doubledealing and hypocrisy.

When the gold rush of 1849 brought tens of thousands of Anglo newcomers into California, Mexicans quickly learned that they had no rights under the treaty. The apparent policy of the United States was to invite all its citizens into the newly annexed territory without regard to the rights of Mexican Americans to the land and property.[30] The natives of the region were soon outnumbered and left to the mercy of the newcomers who considered them as "foreigners" and "greasers." But they were not so despised that their skill and knowledge in prospecting and mining gold were not exploited. How deeply present-day prejudice against Mexicans is rooted is seen from the enactment of the Foreign Miners Tax Law of 1850 which taxed all foreigners working in the gold diggings.[31] The monthly tax was so high that it soon drove away all the Mexican nationals and South Americans as well as Mexican Americans. Mexicans were hated because of a general hatred for the "greaser" nation of Mexico and the war which had inflamed feelings against all things Mexican (many of the argonauts were Mexican War veterans). Ironically the exclusion of Mexican miners had an extremely adverse effect on Anglo business. With the Mexicans gone, the businessmen lost some of their best paying customers.[32]

The greatest land grab since the dispossession of the American Indians robbed Mexican *ricos* of their rightful property despite the treaty's provisions. Through litigation, legislation, financial maneuvering, and manipulation, the Spanish-speaking were soon dispossessed of their *ranchos* and other land holdings. The Gwin Act of 1851 stated that a board of three commissioners would decide the validity of land claims. The claimant and government had the right to appeal to the Supreme Court if they disputed the board's decisions. Many Mexicans lost their lands by their being declared invalid; others lost theirs by the titles' being disputed, winning their claims in the courts but ultimately losing all in attorneys' fees. Shrewd and unscrupulous Yankee lawyers managed to get control over thousands of acres by playing "benefactor" and legal counselor to many of the Mexican landowners and selling them out to the highest bidder or managing affairs so that they themselves got possession of the land titles.[33]

Mexicans fared no better on the political scene.[34] As early as 1856 *gringo* Democratic bosses called a special convention in Los Angeles to consider splitting the county in two as a means to increase the *gringo* influence in the town's election. This was the beginning of the gerrymandering which endures to this day. Open racism was a big factor in the election of 1856 in which a Mexican ran and was defeated by a *gringo* newcomer. In California some of the native Californians ran for office and were elected, but they were relatively small in number and influence. Actually the *gringos* were simply giving token and symbolic leadership roles to a few men who had formerly been part of the Mexican power structure prior to the conquest. New Mexico was one of the former Mexican provinces which had a minimum of Anglo immigrants from the United States and was able to keep political control in many areas. This is the reason that statehood was denied for so long to New Mexico. Apparently the Mexicans outnumbered the Anglos and therefore it was assumed inadvisable to grant "full civil rights to a people largely illiterate and of an alien culture."[35]

If today in the Southwest the education of the Spanish-surnamed is tragically and woefully inadequate, the reasons lie buried deep in the past. Mexicans were guaranteed by treaty that their education would be protected, an education suited to the distinct cultural and linguistic needs of the children. Yet from the beginning of *gringo* rule, no Spanish language instruction was ever adequately provided.[36] It has been said that the coming of the Anglo ushered in the age of public school education for all children. Such a statement should be amended to state "all children *except* Mexicans." The American public school system did nothing for the Mexican children. One searches in vain to find Spanish surnames on public school rolls in the Southwest after the war. The Mexican children were discouraged from attending by the failure to provide instruction for them. The children stayed home. This is the genesis of the Chicano high school dropouts and flunkouts of today.

In 1855 the Bureau of Public Instruction in California ordered that all schools must teach exclusively in English.[37] There were attempts at Spanish-language instruction in some communities where Mexicans were still strong politically and by some individuals who had the welfare of the children at heart. These attempts failed because of the school board's opposition and the nativist sentiment among Anglos. In Los Angeles in 1855 there were 500 school-age children who spoke Spanish. Classes in Spanish were begun, but when funds from the public treasury ran out nothing was done by officials to revive the program and the children's education ended.[38] It is to the credit of the Catholic Church that it tried to assume the duties of the state; the parochial school system in Southern California began as a reaction to the Yankee exclusion of Spanish-speaking children from the schoolroom.[39]

The Chicano community today has made serious charges of injustice and repression by the American system of law enforcement and criminal justice. These feelings within the Chicano community did not begin during the 1930s or 1940s but began with the occupation of the Southwest. It is remarkable how startling and dramatic a transformation many Mexicans underwent with the changing of the old order. Violence and crime became a way of life for countless young Mexican Americans. Much of this was due to social changes taking place in both the United States and Mexico. But it is also true that these young men turned to a life of crime in reaction to injustices which they felt were being committed against them and their people. They were also keenly aware that their country had been provoked into an unjust war fought solely for the purpose of land acquisition—their land! And without their birthright of land, without any hope of assimilating into the system which disparaged Mexicans, they took to a life of crime to win back pieces of their stolen heritage and to avenge injustices.

The Spanish-speaking felt abandoned and betrayed, sold out by their own country Mexico.[40] Years after the conquest, Mexicans left in the newly annexed states referred to themselves as "our brothers who were sold." They had been sold out by their Mexican brothers and led to the fleecing and slaughter by their American conquerors. The younger Mexicans bitterly resented it and chose the path of rebellion. Three alternatives lay before them: assimilation into the mainstream of Yankee culture and society; passive acceptance of Mexican society (which was now one of conquered people without rights); or armed resistance to what was happening to the old order. The first option was impossible; the second would have been to admit defeat (which many people did); the third was to many the only honorable and acceptable option.

History is studded with the names of such men as Juan Flores, Pancho Daniel, Tiburcio Vasquez, and the legendary Joaquin Murietta. Tiburcio Vasquez was the scourge of many *gringos* until he was finally caught and hanged. When asked for the motives of his life of crime, Vasquez said he had only tried to avenge Yankee injustices committed against his people. "I believed we were being unjustly deprived of the social rights that belonged to us," said Vasquez.[41] In Texas, Juan Nepomucena Cortina, the "Robin Hood of the Rio Grande," was the personification of anti-*gringo* feelings among all Mexican people. Cortina came from wealthy and aristocratic stock but had associated with *vaqueros* and *pelados* from his earliest youth. Many of his friends had bitter grievances against the *gringos,* and Cortina became their champion. In the late 1850s he tried to "liberate" the town of Brownsville and provoked the wrath of the United States Army and the Texas Rangers. Cortina was never captured and for a time issued anti-*gringo* proclamations from across the border where he took refuge.[42]

Vigilantism was the reaction to Mexican lawlessness. Lynch law spread its terror and killing everywhere. Despite the official records, Mexicans were not the only criminals of the time. But always, then as now, Mexicans were the first and often the only ones to be caught and punished. Retaliation was swift whether in court or at the hands of a vigilante mob. A great number of Mexicans were punished by whipping, branding, ear cropping, deportation, or hanging. It is impossible to overestimate the violence at this time in American history; overt violence—lynchings, murders, deportations, border warfare that involved the U.S. Army, et cetera—far greater and more devastating than even that experienced by blacks in the post–Civil War South.

American hatred of Mexicans reached its symbolic climax (symbolic because the actual killings would continue well into the twentieth century) in the hanging of a pregnant Mexican woman in Downieville, California, in 1851. The beautiful Juanita had stabbed an American miner who tried to break into her cabin one night when he was returning home from a boisterous drinking party celebrating the Fourth of July. The miner was drunk. In a fit of anger Juanita killed the man who tried to break down her door and enter. A local physician pleaded in her behalf before a hastily convened kangaroo court of drunken miners, but to no avail. That she was the only woman—and a Mexican woman—to be hanged in the California mining era is an instance pointing not to Mexican criminality or depravity but to how low *gringo* lawlessness and immorality had sunk.[43]

Mexicans in the Southwest felt oppressed by a double standard of justice. Why were only Mexicans being lynched or punished? they asked. The introduction of Anglo law and the repeal of all Mexican laws (publication of the laws in Spanish was also banned) did little to help a deteriorating situation and only generated more feelings of alienation among Mexicans. Insult was added to injury when in 1855 a California law prohibiting vagrancy was passed; it was popularly called the "Greaser law" because the word "greaser" actually appeared in its text.[44] By 1856, Los Angeles was split along racial lines, and Anglos carried sidearms or rifles because they felt the Mexicans in their midst would turn to revolution at any moment.[45] A local Spanish-language newspaper called the entire system of Anglo justice "hypocritical, unfair, and even brutal to the Spanish-speaking."[46]

In the *barrios* of Los Angeles today, and throughout the entire Southwest, nothing has changed since 1856. After generations of mob violence, bloodshed, injustice, and broken promises, Mexicans remain a conquered people. The pattern of oppression remains the same: Chicanos are still being forced to drop out of schools that refuse to meet their educational needs; *barrios* remain gerrymandered and politically impotent; police still stand guard in the *barrios* as if they expected the outbreak of another Mexican revolution; and racial slurs and stereotypes are as current today as ever.

And for generations Anglos refused to honor our accomplishments in their history books or customs because they believed nonwhites, especially Mexicans who were identified with Indian peasants and manual laborers, had nothing to offer history or culture. So Anglos invented a "Spanish" history which was more fantasy than history. It emphasized early mission days when the *padres* took care of their Indian charges and white-skinned Spaniards explored the borderlands in preparation for the coming of the *gringo*. But the truth could not be ignored forever. We rose up ourselves and said, *¡Ya basta!* Enough!

In Mexico, millions proudly assert their *mestizo* blood and boast of being Moctezuma's children and the spiritual heirs of Cuahtémoc. And in conquered Mexico, we have begun to call ourselves *Chicanos* to identify with the very least of the *raza,* and have once again given our conquered land its ancient name, *Aztlan,* the name of the northern Aztec kingdom which today signifies solidarity not only with our brothers who were sold during the Mexican War but also with the Mexican Indian whom the Spaniard never defeated, who lives on in the *Mexicanos* and Mexican Americans of today.

Who are the Mexican American people?

La Raza!
Mejicano!
Español!
Latino!
Hispano!
Or whatever I call myself,
I look the same
I feel the same
I cry
and
Sing the same
I am the masses of my people and
I refuse to be absorbed. . . .
The odds are great
but my spirit is strong
My faith unbreakable
My blood is pure
I am Aztec Prince and Christian Christ
I SHALL ENDURE!
I WILL ENDURE![47]

—RODOLFO "CORKY" GONZALES

NOTES

1. Frank Tannenbaum, *Peace by Revolution* (New York: Columbia University Press, 1933), p. 3.

2. Octavio Paz, *The Labyrinth of Solitude* (New York: Grove Press, Inc., 1961), p. 94.

3. George C. Vaillant, *The Aztecs of Mexico* (Baltimore: Penguin Books, 1960), p. 232.

4. *Ibid.*, p. 216.

5. Charles Gibson, *Spain in America* (New York: Harper and Row, 1966), pp. 48–67.

6. Anita Brenner, *Idols Behind Altars* (Boston: Beacon Press, 1970), p. 78.

7. Tannenbaum, *op. cit.*, p. 5.

8. Magnus Morner, "First Meeting of the Races in the Americas," *The Mexican Americans: An Awakening Minority*, edited by Manuel P. Servín (Beverly Hills: Glencoe Press, 1970), p. 8.

9. Tannenbaum, *op. cit.*, p. 6.

10. Woodrow Borah, *Race and Class in Mexico* (Center for Latin American Studies, Institute of International Studies, University of California, Berkeley, Reprint No. 294), pp. 331–342.

11. John Francis Bannon, *The Spanish Borderlands Frontier: 1513–1821* (New York: Holt, Rinehart, and Winston, 1970), pp. 8–27.

12. Gabriel Marcella, "Spanish-Mexican Contributions to the Southwest," *The Journal of Mexican American History* (Vol. I, Fall 1970), pp. 1–11.

13. William Shepherd, "The Spanish Heritage in America," *A Documentary History of the Mexican Americans*, edited by Wayne Moquin and Charles Van Doren (New York: Praeger Publishers, 1971), pp. 267–270.

14. Joseph H. L. Schlarman, *Mexico, A Land of Volcanoes* (Milwaukee: Bruce Publishing Co., 1950), p. 279.

15. Leonard Pitt, *The Decline of the Californios* (Berkeley and Los Angeles: University of California Press, 1970), pp. 14–17.

16. David T. Leary, "Race and Regeneration," in *The Mexican-Americans: An Awakening Minority*, p. 18.

17. *Ibid.*, p. 25.

18. *Ibid.*, p. 21.

19. *Ibid.*, p. 26.

20. *Ibid.*, p. 27.

21. Pitt, *op. cit.*, p. 283.

22. *The Other Side, or Notes for the History of the War Between Mexico and the United States*, edited and translated by A. C. Ramsey (New York: John Wiley, 161 Broadway, 1850), pp. 19–32.

23. *Ibid.*

24. Otis A. Singeltary, *The Mexican War* (Chicago: The University of Chicago Press, 1960), pp. 71–101.

25. *Ibid.*, p. 70.

26. *Ibid.*, p. 159.

27. Feliciano Rivera, *A Mexican American Source Book* (Menlo Park, California: Educational Consulting Associates, 1970), p. 185.

28. *Ibid.*

29. *Ibid.*, pp. 185–186.

30. Pitt, *op. cit.*, p. 296.

31. *Ibid.*, pp. 60–69.

32. *Ibid.*, p. 65.

33. *Ibid.*, p. 91.

34. *Ibid.*, pp. 198–200.

35. Carey McWilliams, *North from Mexico* (Westport, Conn.: Greenwood Press, 1968—originally published in 1948), p. 52.

36. Pitt, *op. cit.*, pp. 224–228.

37. *Ibid.*, p. 226.

38. *Ibid.*, p. 226.

39. *Ibid.*, pp. 224–228.

40. *Ibid.*, p. 117.

41. McWilliams, *op. cit.*, p. 130.

42. Clarence C. Clendenen, *Blood on the Border* (London: The Macmillan Co., 1969), pp. 16–42.

43. McWilliams, *op. cit.*, pp. 127–128.

44. Pitt, *op. cit.*, p. 198.

45. *Ibid.*, p. 162.

46. *Ibid.*, p. 189.

47. Last stanza from Rodolfo "Corky" Gonzales' epic poem "I Am Joaquin" (privately printed, 1967), p. 20.

CHAPTER THREE

Los Enganchados

THE CONFLICT between *gringos* and Chicanos has raged to the present day. The conflict—mainly economic in nature—began when Mexicans were robbed of their lands and property and were disparaged as racial and cultural inferiors. The pattern of violence has continued without interruption. At times the battle was waged with guns, bombs, and strike-breaking police. Most of the time it has been the overwhelming power of institutions that has controlled and manipulated—with no less a deadly violence—the lives of our people. We have been the unwilling victims in this unequal struggle.

With all odds against us, we have faced powerful *gringo* institutions and, despite heroic efforts, lost the economic battle. The effects of this economic oppression have been profoundly social in nature and account for the Mexican community's poverty, political powerlessness, and generally low status. "History has made economic exploitation by American interests the lot of the Mexican people both north and south of the border," wrote Isabel Gonzalez. "Powerful interests like the Great Western Sugar Company, the greatest importer of Mexican labor, the railroads, the mining and lumbering industries, the cotton and fruit growers, and the cattle and sheep industries have succeeded in keeping the Mexican the most underpaid and oppressed worker so that they will always have a surplus of cheap labor."[1]

I

Cuando salimos de El Paso
A las dos de la mañana,
Le pregunté al reenganchista,
Si vamos para Louisiana.

When we left El Paso
At two in the morning,
I asked the boss contractor
If we are going to Louisiana.

Llegamos a la Laguna
Sin esperanza ninguna.
Le pregunté al reenganchista
Si vamos para "Oclajuma."

We arrived at Laguna
Without any hope.
I asked the boss
If we are going to Oklahoma.

Unos descargaban rieles
Otros descargaban "tallas."
Y otros de los compañeros
Echaban de mil malallas.

Some unloaded rails
And others unloaded ties.
And others of my companions
Threw thousands of curses.

Mas valiera estar en Kansas
Que nos mantenga el gobierno.
Valía mas estar en Juarez
Aunque sea sin trabajar

"It would be better to be in Kansas
Where the government would maintain us."
"It would be better to be in Juarez
Even if we were without work."

Estos versos son compuestos
por un pobre Mexicano
Pa ponerlos al corriente
Del sistema americano.[2]

These verses were composed
By a poor Mexican
To spread the word about
The American system.[2]

Sixty years ago, during the period of heaviest Mexican immigration to the United States, the above song (quoted in part) was sung by the migrants. It was called *"Los Enganchados,"* the hooked ones. And it is no surprise that they would think of themselves in those terms. Just as Mexicans were manipulated and exploited by the Spaniards, those who traveled north in this century would be subjected to still another kind—*"del sistema americano."* Mexican *campesinos* served American interests as perfect models of "economic man,"[3] stripped of their humanity, used for one purpose alone: cheap labor.

An intensive, steady stream of immigrants crossed the border in a relatively short time. Millions came to join their long-separated brethren, descendants of early pioneers who had settled the land long before the *gringo* came. Unlike their predecessors, the latter-day Mexican immigrants did not find a barren wilderness to civilize but a great economic empire in its initial stages of development. Suddenly minerals, lumber, cotton, corn, sheep, cattle, vegetables, and fruits became multimillion (today multibillion) dollar industries. Agriculture, for instance, became a vast "Agribusiness" controlled by corporate farms which supply the nation with nearly half its food. Mexican laborers supplied the essential muscle and sweat in building this massive empire of power, wealth, and productivity.

Who were the immigrants? In the distorted view of many *gringos,* they were short, dark-skinned peasants who anxiously crossed the border to meekly accept whatever unjust fate awaited them. A totally different view is taken by those who actually participated in the history of immigration. The *rucos* in the *barrios* tell a different story. They were sons of the Mexican revolution. They and their fathers did not simply watch history move past them but shaped and created it. They were real men. "Twice in exactly one hundred years Mexico was shaken by uprisings of the dispossessed," wrote Ernesto Galarza, who came to the United States from Mexico with his family. "In 1810 and again in 1910 the revolution was one of people wanting in, not out; they fought to regain possession of the ground they lived on. Migration came only after defeat, . . ."[4]

Mexicans were anything but meek and passive as they revolted in 1810 against the iron rule of Spain. Dominated by the idea that they owned the land they had toiled on from time immemorial, an army of tattered, illiterate peasants, led by the Catholic priest Miguel Hidalgo, had ousted the Spaniards from Mexico. But independence meant little to the average *campesino* while political leaders struggled for personal power and the basic inequalities in land and wealth distribution went unchanged. As a result, Mexicans, following the leadership of Emiliano Zapata, Pancho Villa, and Francisco Madero, revolted again in 1910. Mexico was thrown into another fierce and bloody revolution which was to last for ten long years. Migration came in the wake of their heroic struggle for liberty and land.

Mexican immigration steadily mounted and reached a peak during the twenties as the "push" of internal strife and the "pull" of American labor needs brought nearly half a million across the border.[5] The United States looked to Mexico for labor because European and Asiatic immigration sources had been stemmed by the start of World War I. Mexican dictator Porfirio Diaz and foreign capital had built railroads that enabled mass transportation from deep within Mexico's interior, the *Mesa central* (Michoacan, Guanajuato, et cetera) to the Southwestern United States. Many of the immigrants had been part of a twelve-million–member labor force bound to the soil of the rich *haciendas* in debt-peonage. Their revolution freed them and many moved north. Within thirty years, more than a million Mexicans entered the United States legally and probably more than ten million entered clandestinely. Mexico was drained of nearly ten percent of her population, while on the other side of the border the Mexican population swelled to three times its original size.

The immigration pattern they formed was varied and complex. Some were rural peasants; others came from urban or semiurban areas. Some came as single working men; others came in families. Many living close to the border were able to pass back and forth on temporary jobs; still others came from the interior, and their move involved more of a commitment to stay for a while. Most came to see if they would like the new country and if not they would return. That many chose this option can be seen from the verses of a song composed by Mexican *betabeleros* (sugar-beet workers) who had traveled to Michigan and found that the labor contractor had deceived them:

Yo me quiero regresar	I want to return
Por que no nos han cumplido	Because they haven't done for us
Lo que fueron a contar.	What they said they would.
Aqui vienen y les cuentan	Here they come and they tell you
Que se vayan para allá	That you ought to go up there
Por que allá les tiene todo	Because there you will have everything
Que no van a batallar.	Without having to fight for it.
Pero son puras mentiras	But these are nothing but lies
Los que vienen y les dicen.[6]	And those who come and say those things are liars.[6]

II

THE VAST MAJORITY of immigrants was immediately segregated into certain types of employment by American business concerns. Jobs were principally in large-scale industries, railroads, smelters, copper mines, sugar-beet refineries, and agriculture.[7] For instance, from 1900 to 1921 forty percent of the nation's fruit and truck crops were produced by a labor force comprised of sixty-five to eighty-five percent Mexicans. Mexicans also accounted for sixty percent of the labor in mining industries and between sixty and ninety percent of the section and extra gangs on eighteen western railroads.[8] They were paid less than Anglos and usually given the lowest dead-end jobs available. Many unions made it their official policy to exclude Mexicans; the best-paying jobs were monopolized for union members, all of whom were white. In short, Mexicans were originally recruited and consistently treated as a *class* of people who would only be given certain types of industrial and agricultural work.[9] This pattern of discrimination against Mexicans as a class still exists.

In his monumental *North from Mexico*, Carey McWilliams cited an example of economic discrimination leveled against Mexicans. By the twenties, hundreds of Mexican workers had been recruited to work in industrial enterprises (such as steel plants) as far away from the Southwest as Chicago, Detroit, Gary, Indiana, and Bethlehem, Pennsylvania. This recruitment was thwarted, however, by both the sugar-beet companies and the Southwestern agricultural interests because they did not want to allow Mexicans to be employed in industry outside their own regional companies. These businesses wanted to completely monopolize this cheap labor source for their own field work and low-skill occupations. Moreover they feared that with increased immigration to the Midwest (where the white domestic labor market would suffer more than in the Southwest) there would be a movement to place a quota on Mexican immigration, thus stemming their cheap labor source. "The doors of Middle Western industrial employment were closed almost as soon as they opened," concluded McWilliams. "And in the Southwest, employment opportunities were restricted by custom, by discrimination, and by other factors, to a few limited types of employments."[10] (This also partly accounts for eighty-five percent of the Mexicans in the United States being concentrated in the Southwest.)

Agriculture was hard work, and Mexicans who for generations had toiled on similar soil and under the same conditions were able to withstand long hours of work under the Texas and California sun. But the most extreme and telling hardship such work inflicted was on the children. One-fourth of the children aged six to nine and four-fifths of the children aged ten to fourteen were in the fields alongside their parents. Nearly all children over fourteen were considered to be regular workers. This work pattern virtually destroyed any educational opportunities available to the children of families employed in agriculture. And what entire families earned by their long hours at work was well below existing poverty-level incomes. In Los Angeles during the early forties, for instance, the median income of Mexican families was $790 a year—$520 less than the government recommended minimum for feeding and housing a family of five.[11] It is important to note that conditions in Los Angeles about that time represented the *highest* standard of living for Mexicans in the Southwest. Obviously the chief reason why Southwestern companies monopolized Mexican workers was not because they were hard working, conscientious, and inured to the region's difficult climate and conditions (which they were) but because large numbers of Mexicans within certain job categories kept the labor supply well ahead of demand and wages could be kept at the extreme minimum.

The clearest example of exploitation was the *Bracero* program that began during World War II. Around 1942 the United States persuaded Mexico to allow American industry to recruit Mexican *braceros* who would make up for the domestic labor shortage during the war years. Most of the *braceros* were recruited for agricultural work, and agribusiness considered them as a form of mechanization—efficient, in good condition, economical to operate, and readily returnable with no strings attached.[12] The *bracero* was viewed as stripped of all political, social, or human reality. He was simply a mechanized worker.

The agreement between the United States and Mexico which was later enacted as Public Law 78 by the U.S. Congress in 1951 stipulated that Mexican labor would be brought to this country if the workers were paid the prevailing wage and the importation of foreign labor would have no adverse effect on the domestic labor market. The program in effect enabled American industry and agribusiness not only to recruit urgently needed workers during wartime but, through powerful lobbies in Washington, to prolong the program for twenty years, during which time the American taxpayer subsidized their labor costs despite an extremely adverse effect on the domestic labor market (principally Mexican American workers).

This pattern emerged during the decades of *bracero* importation: agribusiness representatives would lower wages to domestics in such a way that they would be discouraged from applying, thus creating an artificial labor shortage which, in turn, would require Mexican nationals to be brought into the country at the expense of the government. Within a free labor market, with no real opposition from the workers themselves, business set the wages, hours, conditions, and so on. In many cases the wages paid to the *braceros* remained the same or actually decreased through the years. Somehow growers believed that their profit could be made only by taking it from the wages justly due their workers. About this time Secretary of Labor Arthur J. Goldberg expressed his personal disgust at the absolute power "close to despotism" which was exercised over Mexican laborers by American business interests.[13] As another outraged observer put it: "No class of people or type of worker has been more thoroughly exposed to the raw corporate power of the Western world's capitalistic system than . . . farm workers."[14] That, in a nutshell, is the history of Mexican workers in the United States during this century.

III

THE EFFECT OF IMMIGRATION on Mexican Americans was devastating. The extreme plight of Mexican Americans was largely shaped and determined by the massive, uncontrolled waves of immigration. American business used Mexican laborers to profoundly affect the domestic labor market. Wages were lowered, job opportunities were extremely limited, and the organized labor movement among *Mexicanos* as well as Mexican Americans was violently opposed and crushed at every turn. And just as the many native-born Mexicans were on the verge of economic assimilation, immigration on the scale of millions was brought in by profit-minded enterprises and wiped out the progress that had been made. The newcomers, as George I. Sanchez observed, only added to the "cultural indigestion" which had prevailed since the Mexican War.[14]

Mexican Americans had been displaced persons ever since the Anglo invasion, and immigration only deepened and perpetuated the cultural isolation and discrimination. While Anglo-exploited immigration united the Mexican Americans more closely with their original motherland and culture, it also drove a wedge between all Mexicans in the United States and their right to participate fully in society and enjoy its economic prosperity. Leonard Pitt has noted the striking similarities between today's immigrants who cross the border looking for work and the Mexican miners who came from Mexico to work in the California gold diggings in the 1850s. Anglo discrimination excluded them—and along with them, the native-born Mexican Americans—from the gold fields. Both groups are victimized and controlled by the dominant society motivated only by profit. It was that way in the 1850s and remains the same today—only on a much larger scale.

The immigration issue, unfortunately, has often been used by *gringo* interests to divide the Mexican community, setting Chicano against *Mexicano*. Business, labor, and government leaders say that stronger laws are needed to keep "illegal aliens" out of the labor market. Chicanos are deceived into believing that their economic woes have been caused by the "wetback" problem. Nothing could be further from the truth. But what is true is that the *Mexicano* has been used by American business to lower everyone's wages. It is not the Mexican on either side of the border who is the problem. The problem is American industry which has used the Mexicans for its own advantage. Chicanos and *Mexicanos* working together against the *sistema* are more likely to produce real solutions to economic problems than passing laws which would strengthen the Border Patrol or sanction those who enter this country without papers. (According to Bert Corona, half of César Chavez's United Farm Workers Union is composed of *Mexicanos* without papers.)

Before the immigration waves flooded the Southwest in this century, one of the most prominent characteristics of the Mexican American people was their diversity. *Nuevo Mexi-*

canos, Tejanos, and *Californios* greatly differed from one another psychologically, socially, and politically. The New Mexicans were not only surrounded by Apaches and thus isolated from the rest of the Southwest, they were also isolated from each other by mountains and rivers. Moreover, they were bound to an extremely poor soil, and it was necessary to join together in *ejidos* for mutual cooperation and aid. The *Californios,* on the other hand, were *vaqueros,* the West's original cowboys, who raised cattle on the sprawling *ranchos* owned by the *ricos.* The *Tejanos* were poor cousins to the others because for more than one hundred years they had manned lonely, barren outposts largely neglected by Mexico. The many differences of the colonies were created out of differing needs and conditions and produced a highly diverse people.

The Mexicans came from widely varied backgrounds—rural and urban, "ancient" and modern, unassimilated and assimilated. World War II and the draft system brought many of them together for the first time. Raúl Morín described what must have taken place in countless army induction centers and training camps:

> Here were all types of raw recruits. They came from farms, from large cities, from small villages, from the backwoods, and from the hills—from all parts of the United States and from some parts of Mexico. They had been laborers, small businessmen, farmers, truck drivers, craftsmen, students and just plain *vagos* (vagrants).
>
> . . . The names most often repeated, when they were together, were those of the many small barrios and suburbs which many called home. . . . Such places as *Maravilla, Chiques* (Oxnard), Simons, Jim-town, Limonera, Sespe, San Antonio's "Westside," *Calle Ancha* in Austin, "Magnolia" in Houston, Bessemer in Pueblo, "Larrimer," in Denver, *El Pachuco, Juariles, La Daisey, El Dorado, El Ranchito,* Chinatown, and *El Hoyo* were well represented. . . .
>
> One could always tell where they came from by their manner of speech (when they expressed themselves). It was quite easy to distinguish the fast-English-talking Angelenos from the slow-Spanish-

talking Texan or New Mexican. The *Caló* talk (slang talk) of the border inhabitant from El Paso and Juarez was in contrast to the homespun Spanish of the Coloradoan or Arizonan.[15]

Besides reinforcing isolation for years to come, immigration tended to divide Mexicans from one another. As a result of discrimination toward *Mexicanos* (foreign born) the older inhabitants became defensive about their own identity and consequently denied the ancient blood ties with the *Mexicanos* by calling themselves "Spanish Americans." Similarly in Texas, where Mexicans were so disparaged and reviled that "Mexican" became synonymous with "dirty" or "inferior," many Mexican Americans began to call themselves "Latin Americans." These changes in name were adopted around 1927, just as immigration had created a significant presence of *Mexicanos* in the Southwest.[16]

In California, where "Mexican" also became a dirty word, the myth of "early Spanish days" replaced the factual historical record of Mexican settlement and tradition. In an interview conducted by Celia Heller with Joe Valdez (fictitious name), a nineteen-year-old high school graduate working as a dental technician, the tendency to deny racial heritage is well illustrated:

> I work in Beverly Hills. I went to cash my check in a bank. There was a lady there: her name was Vargas. And I don't know what got into me. Instead of asking her whether she is Mexican I asked her: "Are you Spanish?" She got kind of annoyed. "No," she said. "I'm Mexican." It was kind of shocking. I got thinking. I asked her if she was Spanish; deep inside I didn't want to hurt her feelings (by asking her if she was Mexican). I thought about it and I felt like a fool. She said, "No, I'm Mexican." Just like that.[17]

While some Mexican Americans may have denied their racial heritage in an attempt to distinguish themselves from the newcomers, Anglos saw little difference between the two groups and discriminated against them equally. They were poor together! For instance, three-fourths of all Mexicans in the United States live in *barrios*.[18] And *barrios* exist because of economic discrimination. Most sprang up forty and fifty years ago, usually in an unincorporated area and invariably on the wrong side of something. Most "Spic-towns" or "Mex-towns" loudly proclaimed what their clear purpose and function was in Anglo terms: to isolate and contain Mexican people in a position of economic servitude and social disadvantage.

In Maravilla Park (East Los Angeles) where many of the first immigrants to Los Angeles settled, most of the families lived in shacks built of scrap lumber and boxes. Only ten of the three hundred and seventeen dwellings had cesspools with flush toilets connected to them.[19] The men, when fortunate enough to find employment, were listed as unskilled laborers. Health and living conditions were deplorable; infant mortality was extremely high, and the tuberculosis rate was the scourge of the community. Racial discrimination in schools, recreational facilities, and public services was widespread.[20] Theaters, barber shops, swimming pools, et cetera were closed to Mexicans. But for all its anti-Mexican ways, Los Angeles was actually a *better* place for *raza* to live than anywhere else in the Southwest.

One of the most tragic chapters in Mexican American history, where both *Mexicanos* and Chicanos suffered together, was the mass deportations during the 1930s. By the time of the Great Depression many Mexican immigrants had settled permanently in Texas, Arizona, and California. Some intermarried with Mexican Americans, others came with their families from Mexico, and still others married immigrants like themselves whom they met in the United States. At this time, the overwhelming majority of Mexicans in the United States were foreign born, but, of course, any children born in the United States would be American citizens entitled to all the rights of citizenship. The Depression created widespread unemployment, and the heavy burden of welfare relief rested directly on the local level (the federal government offered no aid at this time). As a result of economic crisis, many communities came up with the idea of "repatriating" their Mexican welfare recipients or any Mexican who might be likely to become a burden on the community. While some Mexicans returned to Mexico of their own free will, most were sent back against their will or pressured to return. Emory S. Bogardus wrote:

> Many Mexican immigrants are returning to Mexico under a sense of pressure. They fear that all welfare aid will be withdrawn if they do not accept the offer to help them out of our country. In fact, some of them report that they are told by public officials that if they do not accept the offer to take them to the border no further welfare aid will be given them and that their record will be closed with the notation, "Failed to cooperate."[21]

There was an important economic aspect to this; it was found that Mexicans could be shipped back to the capital of Mexico in wholesale lots for $14.70 per person. This sum was less than a week's welfare costs in room and board.[22] Besides saving money, welfare officials and others believed that Mexicans would be better off or happier in Mexico. As a result, more than 312,000 persons were deported. Whole families were summarily notified and told to pack all their belongings for the long train ride back "home." More than half of the Mexicans who were deported were *American citizens.*[23]

The gross injustice of deporting American citizens and Mexican nationals against their will indicates how the rights of Mexicans in the United States were completely disregarded. The illegal actions of welfare officials and other government agencies only served to reinforce the mistrust felt by Mexicans toward institutions that purported to protect and serve the people. In times of prosperity the Mexican was welcomed into this country as a low-wage laborer in the fields or mines, but in time of economic hardship he was thrown out of the country. Mexicans, as Armando Morales has observed, were literally railroaded out of American society.

IV

In the nineteenth century Mexicans in the Southwest were caricatured as "ignorant and degraded animals" by *gringos* who wished to justify the American invasion of Mexican territory. The early pattern and function of anti-Mexican prejudice continued into the twentieth century. When confronted with the glaring symptoms of economic discrimination against Mexicans, the typical response was to view Mexicans as the *kind* of people who deserved what they got. They were too "dirty," "diseased," or "lazy" to keep up their homes and communities. In a government-sponsored report in 1930 the tuberculosis rate of Mexicans in California was attributed to Mexicans' being of "fundamentally less sturdy stock." This excuse, based on stereotypes, conveniently absolved the dominant group of having caused the conditions or having responsibility to do something about the conditions.[24] According to Gordon Allport's definition, a stereotype is an "exaggerated belief associated with a category. Its *function* (emphasis mine) is to justify our conduct in relation to that category."[25] The images of the Mexican as "dirty," "violent," "innately weak," "culturally deprived," et cetera were all part of a complex rationale to justify and maintain the economic and social advantages which the dominant group enjoyed at the Mexican's expense.

Traditionally, therefore, Mexicans have been viewed in this country as a "problem." This *gringo* response assumes that the Mexican, by his cultural, linguistic, or mental "handicaps," is responsible for being a burden on the rest of society. In keeping with this problem approach, many Americans, especially those descended from European immigrants in this century, argue that if the Poles, Irish, and Italians could make it in America, then Mexicans also could have pulled themselves up by their own bootstraps. If Mexicans haven't made good by this time, they explain, maybe it's because Mexicans are low achievers by nature or culture.

The critics ignore history. They don't realize how old

La Raza really is. (The average Chicano in East L.A. is only seventeen years old, but in reality he is as old as Cuahtémoc or Felipe de Neve.) Mexicans did not immigrate to this country, but have been constantly at odds with those who did—the *gringos.* Low achievers? They created a civilization which made the Spaniards gasp with wonder and excitement. And in the Southwest, they established their own economy, culture, laws, language, and educational system. They had a well-developed society with *rico,* middle, and lower classes; they were autonomous. At least until the *gringo* came. Anglo immigrants by the hundreds of thousands swept into the region after the war. They refused to acknowledge the existence of Mexicans as a distinct ethnic group with a unique cultural identity.* The result of this refusal has led George I. Sanchez to sadly observe that Mexicans remained unassimilated by "default," i.e., the United States failed to Americanize the Spanish-speaking in those areas where they lived in great numbers.[26]

At the time of annexation, most Mexicans (like most people everywhere else) were illiterate. They were isolated and their cultural ties with Mexico had been severed and would remain so until the next century. It would have been relatively easy for the institutions of social incorporation to reach out and bring the Mexican, especially the children, into the mainstream of the new American culture and society. But the United States merely coexisted with their newly adopted Mexican American citizens who, in lieu of any other alternative, tenaciously clung to their language and culture to offset the dislocation of annexation. And to the Americans, theirs was the culture and language of a conquered people.

*Not until 1970 were Mexican Americans officially held to be an "identifiable ethnic group" (*Cisneros v. Corpus Christi Independent School District,* Civil Action No. 68-C-95; June 4, 1970). We had to prove in a court of law that we are brown! This enabled Chicanos for the first time to invoke, as a visible minority like black Americans, the provisions of the Civil Rights Act of 1964, et cetera.

At the beginning of this century, when Mexicans moved northward in great numbers, they did not follow the European model of immigration. Italians, Poles, and Irish had few regrets in leaving their homeland or at least were committed to giving up their land for another by crossing an ocean. But Mexicans, who were so close to Mexico and found so much of Mexico in the *barrios,* did not have to change their attitudes radically in moving a few hundred miles to the north. Even the jobs they found in agriculture, mining, sheep, and cattle raising had all been pioneered and established by their forebears centuries earlier. Mexicans had a historical, cultural, and geographical affinity for the region.

And Mexican immigration, incredible as it may seem, bears a closer resemblance to the black slave trade than to European immigration. Mexicans were recruited to work in the United States, not to settle down and be accepted into society. Many employers thought that their workers went back to Mexico after the season was over; they overlooked the fact that more and more were establishing themselves in the cities where they lived during the off-season. The low-skill labor source which the Mexican immigrants represented was not replaced by other immigrant groups, whereas successive waves of European immigration kept the newest arrivals at the bottom of the wage scale while the others moved up. Mexican laborers were continually joined and reinforced in their servitude by other Mexicans, and the vicious cycle of poverty and deprivation was established.

Finally, the nature of the United States–Mexico border accounts for so many of the unique aspects of Mexican immigration. "There is no border to many of our people," says one Chicano leader in East L.A. "There is no border in their hearts."[27] The border was not the result of cultural or geographical differences but was imposed by conquest in 1848 and later by outright purchase in 1853 (the Gadsden Purchase obtained an additional 45,532 square miles). The border cut Mexico in half and created impossible problems for both countries. The length of the border stretches nearly

2,000 miles from Brownsville to San Diego and enables Mexicans to cross without detection. The border mainly follows the Rio Grande (which in certain places is dry all the time!). People are not separated by the border, as McWilliams has observed; they are drawn together.[28] Communities and *families* which were united were suddenly cut in half by the United States–imposed border. For instance Laredo and Nuevo Laredo, El Paso and Ciudad Juarez, Brownsville and Matamoros are really arbitrary halves of originally whole and integral Mexican communities. (That is why, moreover, the Chicano's economic troubles can't be solved by stopping his "wetback" brothers, cousins, uncles, and aunts from coming across the border. That's only half the picture. Economic problems, especially the wage problem, can only be solved by both the United States and Mexico working together to stabilize conditions and wages on *both* sides of the border.)

V

> . . . We have gone before the courts, we have set up picket lines, and last night we marched right down Broadway from Olympic to the Federal Building (in downtown Los Angeles) passing out our leaflets. The people are catching on to the idea of mobilizing themselves, of not being paralyzed with fear. . . . And one of these days you are going to see a demonstration down Broadway of 100,000 of us. Then, who are they going to deport!
>
> —BERT CORONA[29]

POOR PEOPLE have always organized to fight for better living conditions and wages. Chicanos are no exception. Contrary to popular opinion, there is a long history of organization efforts among the Mexican American people. As early as 1883, Mexican agricultural workers (known as "cowboys" at the time) were organized and struck under the leadership of Juan Gomez in Texas.[30] In 1922 Mexican *campesinos* tried to establish a grape-pickers union in Fresno, California.

The first successful union was formed in Southern California in 1927; the *Confederación de Uniones Obreros Mexicanos* had three thousand workers organized into twenty locals in such places as Los Angeles, Garden Grove, Orange, Santa Ana, San Fernando, Anaheim, Santa Monica, Buena Park, La Jolla, et cetera.[31] They struck in the Imperial Valley in 1928, and in 1930 nearly five thousand Mexicans struck again. The second strike was successful until the growers brutally attacked strikers with tear gas, guns, shells, and bombs.[32] In 1933 seven thousand Mexican workers walked out of the berry, onion, and celery fields of Los Angeles County. Later the Cannery and Agricultural Workers Industrial Union, a left-wing group, enlisted several thousand Mexican workers to protest poor housing and to strike against racial discrimination and low pay.[33]

In 1936 two thousand celery workers, all Mexicans, went on strike in Los Angeles County. By midsummer of the same year more than two thousand Mexican strikers tied up for several weeks a twenty million dollar citrus crop in Orange County.[34] Also during the thirties Mexicans were striking in Arizona, New Mexico, Texas, Idaho, Colorado, Washington, and Michigan, as well as in California.[35] Besides agricultural strikes there were strikes among the sheepherders in West Texas, the pecan shellers in San Antonio, and the coal miners in New Mexico.[36] During the forties and fifties the National Farm Workers Union did much organizing among Mexican laborers. And during the sixties, AWOC (Agricultural Workers Organizing Committee, AFL–CIO), an organization composed of many Mexicans, was able to successfully raise farm wages in 1960–1961 as a result of their organized efforts. From 1965 on, the scene has been largely dominated by UFWOC (United Farmworkers Organizing Committee). Obviously, Mexicans have been anything but unorganized for the past seventy years.

Time and again, however, Mexican workers who sought to unionize were at the mercy of powerful business interests. Every attempt to unionize was savagely beaten back by force, intimidation, killings, deportations, and wholesale arrests. But Mexicans were fighters willing to unite in an effort to win better wages and conditions. Little help was forthcoming from organized labor unions; they provided verbal encouragement but very little tangible support.[37] Nevertheless, just as Mexicans had risen up against oppression in Mexico, they also rose up again and again in attempts to unionize themselves in this country. Through their many efforts they became pioneers in the trade union movement, and many of the strikers, who were deported to Mexico, spearheaded the organized labor movement there.[38]

In 1970 César Chavez's UFWOC scored a dramatic victory against almost impossible odds by winning grower recognition of the California farmworkers union. UFWOC is the first effective farmworkers union in history. Three facts should be noted about Chavez's union victory: it can only be understood (and could only have taken place) within the historical context of Mexican labor struggles in the Southwest; Chavez succeeded in part because the U.S. government terminated the *Bracero* program which for more than twenty years had served as an agribusiness subsidy, thus strengthening the domestic labor force's bargaining power; and the primary significance is that it promises to create a new order in farm-labor management relations that will have "humanity as its purpose and the economy as its tool, thus reversing the present order of the system."[39]

The greatest union victories, however, are yet to take place; and they will happen in the cities where eighty percent of the *raza* live. Today, *La Hermandad General de Trabajadores* (General Brotherhood of Workers) in California has organized 31,000 *Mexicano* workers—*Mexicanos* who crossed the border without papers or who were born here yet do not have the documents to prove it. The union was organized in 1968 by Bert Corona, founder and past president of the Mexican American Political Association (MAPA), who currently makes his headquarters at the Centro de Acción Social Autónomo (CASA) in Los Angeles. There are chapters throughout the state (San Fernando, Coachella, Santa Barbara, Livingston, National City, Imperial Valley, et cetera), and in Los Angeles alone there are 10,000 members organized from the *barrios* there. But the union is still short of its organizational goals because there are an estimated 300,000 *Mexicanos* in Los Angeles without papers. Many of them have lived in this country for many years, have paid relatively higher taxes than anyone else, yet are not entitled to draw unemployment compensation, welfare, Social Security benefits (even though Social Security is deducted from their low wages), et cetera. "They are totally vulnerable," says Bert Corona. "If they complain or protest they fear they will be deported."

Still they have overcome the fear of deportation and have joined the *Hermandad* to press for recognition of their rights from employers as well as the United States government, which labels them as "illegal aliens" or "wetbacks." The union has demonstrated, picketed, and used the courts to combat measures like the Dixon-Arnett Bill, which was passed in California recently and which stipulated that employers who knowingly hire "illegal" workers and thus adversely affect the employment of workers who are permanent residents here will be fined from $200 to $500. According to Corona, the bill did more harm than good, causing tens of thousands of *Mexicano* workers to be fired from their jobs. Not only were countless *Mexicanos* fired, but the ones who were able to keep their jobs and the new workers from Mexico who were hired were forced to forfeit $300 of their first wages as a "security deposit" to the boss in case he was caught by the *migra* and fined. (Many *Mexicanos* never got their $300 back, and they were not in a position to complain about it.) It is another tactic to pit Mexican against Mexican and deceive Mexican people and everyone else into believing that so-called wetbacks are responsible for poor living conditions and low wages and unemployment in this country. The union won the court battle and the Dixon-Arnett Law was held unconstitutional in a Los Angeles Superior Court. Similar legislation, however, is now before Congress. *Casa Hermandad* members say that such legislation is the wrong approach to solving problems that have been caused by American businesses and industries that have used both *Mexicanos* and Mexican Americans for their own profit.

Many industries have established twin plants along the border—for example in Calexico, California, and Tecate, Mexico—to utilize cheap Mexican labor. The plant on the American side does the automated work and then ships the unfinished product to the Mexican side, where Mexican labor supplies whatever assembly-line work remains to be done. According to Corona, this is one of the many ways that the meat-packing industries, garment industry, electronics companies like RCA, Motorola, and Packard Bell have lowered wages and kept Mexicans poor on both sides of the border.

"The Man one-upped us again," says Corona. "He planned ahead and saw that we would get organized and so he 're-rationalized,' shifted assembly of his product from a process that would involve much labor—the kind that organized workers can demand four or five dollars an hour to do—to one that is highly automated." *Mexicanos,* many of them without papers, have been brought in to do the work of "re-rationalized" industries which offer the types of jobs and wages that only "totally vulnerable" workers would take.

But the people are organizing and fighting—as they always have. And if the *Hermandad* is as successful in organizing *Mexicano* workers in the coming years as they were from 1968 to 1972, they may indeed be marching down Broadway in downtown Los Angeles—100,000 strong—to protest the shabby treatment, economic discrimination, and denial of basic rights (guaranteed by the Treaty of Guadalupe-Hidalgo!) which have been their lot ever since the first *enganchados* crossed the border.

Today Mexican Americans continue to hold inferior jobs in nearly every major occupational category. Their earnings for these jobs continue to be generally smaller than the wages given to white workers in comparable jobs.[40] The unemployment and underemployment rates continue to be consistently higher for Mexicans than for everyone else (in Los Angeles in 1972 the unemployment rate was 5.9 percent for the general population, while it was 20 percent for the Chicano). A third of all Mexican people live in poverty in this nation, and in terms of per person median income they make forty-seven cents for every Anglo dollar, a rate lower than that for blacks.[41] Low income has led to shabby housing at a rate exceeding that of Anglos and blacks. Education has suffered largely because poor education is the logical consequence of hard-core poverty.

Mexican immigrants who looked for peace and a place to sink their roots ended up as draftees in a vast army of men, women, and children who worked for low wages and no security or future. They have been forced into the lowest place on the economic totem pole so that those at the top could keep bringing in the highest profits at the expense of their workers.[42] Whether they worked in the fields or in the urban sweatshops of "re-rationalized" industries, the results were always the same: job discrimination, poor living conditions, lack of educational opportunities, or inferior, inadequate schools; and always, there was racial prejudice born of hatred, malice, or scorn on the individual level, while on the institutional level, it served to justify and maintain the inequalities of the status quo.

Some progress has been made and Mexican people have been responsible for these gains. But today the picture largely remains bleak.

NOTES

1. Isabel Gonzalez, "Stepchildren of a Nation," in *A Documentary History of the Mexican Americans,* edited by Wayne Moquin (New York: Praeger Publishers, 1971), pp. 321–322.

2. Manuel Gamio, *Mexican Immigration to the United States* (Chicago: University of Chicago, 1930), pp. 84–86.

3. Ernesto Galarza, *Merchants of Labor: The Mexican Bracero Story* (San Jose, California: Rosicrucian Press, 1965), p. 16.

4. *Ibid.*, pp. 20–21. Mr. Galarza reminisces about the Mexican revolution and his family's move to California from Mexico in his autobiographical *Barrio Boy* (Notre Dame: University of Notre Dame Press, 1971).

5. Leo Grebler, Joan W. Moore, Ralph Guzman, *The Mexican American People: The Nation's Second Largest Minority* (New York: The Free Press, 1970), p. 65.

6. Gamio, *op. cit.*, pp. 86–87.

7. Carey McWilliams, *North from Mexico* (New York: Greenwood Press, 1968), p. 215.

8. *Ibid.*, pp. 185–186.

9. *Ibid.*, p. 215.

10. *Ibid.*, pp. 184–185.

11. *The Mexican Americans: An Awakening Minority,* edited by Manuel P. Servín (Beverly Hills: Glencoe Press, 1970), p. 151.

12. *Ramparts* report of September 1965, in Servín, *op. cit.*, p. 188.

13. Quoted in Galarza, *Merchants of Labor*, p. 231.

14. A. V. Krebs, Jr., "Agribusiness in California," *Commonweal* (October 9, 1970), pp. 45–47.

15. Raúl Morín, "Draftees and Volunteers," in Servín, *op. cit.*, pp. 101–102.

16. McWilliams, *op. cit.*, pp. 78–79.

17. Celia S. Heller, "Chicano Is Beautiful," in *Commonweal* (January 23, 1970), pp. 455–456.

18. ———, *Mexican American Youth: Forgotten Youth at the Crossroads* (New York: Random House, 1966), p. 21.

19. Servín, *op. cit.*, p. 151.

20. *Ibid.*, pp. 151–152.

21. Emory S. Bogardus, "Repatriation and Readjustment," in Servín, *op. cit.*, p. 93.

22. Carey McWilliams, "Getting Rid of the Mexican," in *A Documentary History of the Mexican Americans*, p. 298.

23. *Ibid.*, p. 294.

24. "Mexicans in California: A Report of Governor C. C. Young's Fact-Finding Committee," in Servín, *op. cit.*, pp. 82–83.

25. Gordon Allport, *The Nature of Prejudice* (Cambridge: Addison-Wesley, 1954), p. 191.

26. George I. Sanchez, "History, Culture and Education," in *La Raza: Forgotten Americans,* edited by Julian Samora (Notre Dame: University of Notre Dame Press, 1966), p. 23.

27. Comment made by Eduardo Perez, East Los Angeles community worker, quoted in Stan Steiner's *La Raza: The Mexican Americans* (Harper and Row: New York, 1969), p. 125.

28. McWilliams, *North from Mexico,* p. 61.

29. Remark made in a January 22, 1972, speech; in "Bert Corona Speaks" (New York: Pathfinder Press, Inc., 1972), p. 21.

30. McWilliams, *North from Mexico,* p. 190, quoted in Salvador Alvarez "Mexican American Community Organizations," in *Voices: Readings from El Grito,* edited by Octavio Ignacio Romano-V. (Berkeley: Quinto Sol Publications, 1971), p. 91.

31. McWilliams, *ibid.,* p. 191; quoted in Alvarez, *ibid.,* p. 97.

32. McWilliams, *ibid.,* p. 191.

33. *Ibid.*

34. *Ibid.,* p. 192.

35. Octavio Ignacio Romano-V., "The Distortion of Mexican American History," in *El Grito* (Vol. II, No. 1, Fall 1968), p. 15.

36. *Ibid.*

37. Grebler et al., *op. cit.,* p. 94; also Galarza, *Merchants of Labor,* p. 257.

38. McWilliams, *North from Mexico,* pp. 189, 203.

39. Peter Matthiessen, *Sal Si Puedes: Cesar Chavez and the New American Revolution* (New York: Random House, 1969), p. 30.

40. Grebler et al., *op. cit.,* p. 22.

41. *Ibid.,* p. 19.

42. William E. Scholes, "The Migrant Worker," in Samora, *op. cit.,* p. 63.

CHAPTER FOUR

The Barrios of Poverty

I

THE MOST FAMOUS BARRIO, and the largest in the Southwest, is East Los Angeles, where more than half a million Chicanos live. It is easy to get to East L.A. from anywhere else in the city because, in the last few years, four major freeways have plowed through the area, disrupting and displacing *barrio* residents. And there are hundreds of other *barrios* outside East L.A. which have been just as severely scarred by freeway construction, urban renewal, and other less visible forms of economic discrimination. Drive past City Hall in downtown Los Angeles and continue on North Broadway for two miles, and you will find yourself in the Happy Valley *barrio* in the Lincoln Heights district.

Happy Valley is bounded on three sides by rolling hills, and most visitors to the area would probably feel they had been taken back in time sixty years and were in the middle of a small village in rural Mexico instead of five minutes from Los Angeles civic center. The houses, which were constructed in the 1920s, are small, shabby, and overcrowded. In places there are only dirt roads, although the city street maps indicate they are paved. Even where there are some paved roads, often there are no streetlights or sidewalks because the people are too poor to pay the city to have them put in. Most *barrios* are like Happy Valley.

Nothing is new about Mexicans living together in *barrios*. Old Town in Santa Fe, New Mexico, is as old as the *conquistadores* of the sixteenth century. Others like Happy Valley, Chiques (Oxnard), and Santa Paula, in Southern California, are as recent as yesterday's immigrants. Still other *barrios* will be formed by tomorrow's arrivals from Mexico. What is most striking about all of the *barrios* is not the quaint *mañana-siesta* atmosphere romanticized by John Steinbeck in *Tortilla Flat,* but the widespread poverty. *Barrio* poverty is not simply a lack of money or the finer things in life; it is often a lack of aspiration and hope. Those who live in such poverty —and over a third of all Chicanos do—are society's losers. They have no skills, no education, no social influence. For them there is no possible way out of the *barrio*'s culture of poverty.

The *barrio* became a slum and a satellite community of the dominant society after the conquest. Before that time Mexicans had control over their communities. An example of this self-determination was the *ejidos* in New Mexico, where the people owned the land in common and shared their tools, equipment, and resources with one another. When the land was invaded, control was taken from them. And what the invading armies of the United States failed to do with military might was carried out by the imposition of a completely foreign legal, educational, and economic framework, a new language, a new set of values (which did not recognize the New Mexicans' communal land grants), and a new government.

What this sweeping loss of control meant was described by George I. Sanchez in his classic study, *Forgotten People*:

> Unaware of their rights and status as American citizens, and incapable of voicing their views and feelings, they became cannon fodder for political guns. . . . Defenseless before the onslaught of an intangible yet superior force of ruthless politicians and merchants who stole their lands, stock, water rights, the economic foundations of New Mexican life were undermined and began to crumble. . . . The New Mexican knows not how to make his public servants come to his aid. He falls prey to the forces of political exploitation. He succumbs to mistreatment and neglect. In despair, he becomes a fatalist. . . .[1]

The greed and self-interest of a conquering people created the *barrios* as we know them today. That is why they have lost so much of their original beauty and often resemble concentration camps for conquered people.

Sanchez described the rural poverty of Taos, New Mexico, where villagers and farmers live on the extremes of physical degradation and hunger. But it is a mistake to think that, as many of the younger people move off the farms into the cities, they will be better off. Whether they move to Albuquerque, Denver, or Los Angeles, they will find the same culture of poverty, only in an urban setting. In the cities, according to the 1960 U.S. census, more than thirty percent of Mexican American homes or dwellings were overcrowded, broken down, and shabby.[2] In Texas cities, the situation is worse; the overwhelming majority of Mexican families lived in such conditions.[3] In the entire nation, the three poorest cities are not found in the deep South but in Texas: they are San Antonio, El Paso, and Corpus Christi. The poverty of the people is as abject as the *jacales* (shacks made of cardboard boxes and scrap lumber) they are crowded into. Increasingly, Mexicans are moving off the farms to escape poverty only to find it waiting for them in the cities.

And life in the urban *barrios* has added disadvantages. The Chicano is cheated by grocery stores that sell him low-quality food (East L.A. stores sell only commercial grade meat—the lowest quality for human consumption) at extremely high prices. He is cheated by furniture and appliance stores that often charge him nearly twice as much as he would pay elsewhere. He is discriminated against by car dealers for the sole reason that he is a Mexican. And banks in the *barrio* refuse to lend him money at acceptable interest rates. Although it is hard to document the actual extent of economic exploitation in the *barrio,* the preceding conclusions were proven to exist in a recent study of two representative neighborhoods in East L.A.[4]

Most businesses in East L.A. are housed in old buildings in need of renovation or a "face lift," and inside are poorly lit, cluttered, and unattractive. Not at all like modern suburban department stores. The businesses are not run by Mexican Americans but usually by Oriental or Jewish people. But the clerks speak Spanish and the stores carry Mexican food, newspapers, et cetera. Mexican people, who need cultural reinforcement, are thus drawn to these businesses; but it is no more than a lure because the stores charge higher prices, have higher credit rates, and offer inferior goods.

In his field research, Sturdivant, who conducted the study, used teams of Mexican American and Anglo-white couples who visited the same stores, asked for the same merchandise, and presented the same credit references and financial profile. All the couples found that prices were much higher than those in the control area (an Anglo-white middle class neighborhood which was contrasted with East L.A.). For instance, an Olympic color console TV sold for $700 in East L.A. but only $630 in the control area. A gas range sold for $200 in East L.A. but for only $110 in the control area.[5] In many of the stores the Mexican American couples were charged higher prices than their Anglo counterparts. Couples visited eight East L.A. auto dealers and found that the Mexican American couples were not only asked to pay a higher overall price for a given car but also a grossly unfair interest rate (12 percent) in comparison with their Anglo-white counterparts (8 percent).[6]

In the Anglo-white neighborhood, the control area, it was found that Mexican American couples were still exploited. They were given "special" treatment by being asked to pay $119 for a 19-inch RCA television set while their Anglo counterparts—with the same credit and financial profile—were asked to pay only $109. When an 18-month contract was drawn up, the overall price for the Mexican American couple was $169 but only $122 for the Anglos.[7] No matter where they turn, Chicanos can count on being cheated.

Political powerlessness is another characteristic of *barrio* life. People have no say in what happens to their neighborhood. Freeways, new housing developments (not for Chicanos), or shopping centers are planned by urban renewal commissions established by local or state government, but the people who are directly displaced are never consulted. Without notice or a hearing they are driven from their homes and neighborhoods. Relocation agencies are set up, but what can replace a man's neighbors of twenty years, or a movie house which shows Spanish-language films, or the local *cantina?* The situation has prompted Ernesto Galarza to say: "What was accomplished between 1850 and 1880 by the United States cavalry, legal chicanery, tax frauds and treaty violations, is now carried forward by . . . urban renewal."[8] Protests are futile. In most cases the people raise no protest because they have no experience in such matters.

Galarza, with Herman Gallegos and Julian Samora, conducted a two-year study for the Ford Foundation, analyzing the *barrio* situation. Their conclusions are not promising. Cities have outgrown themselves and are straining under the pressure of ever-increasing population. Into the complex and rapidly changing urban situation come more and more displaced Mexicans to join the ranks of the hard-core unemployed. In California most of the Mexican population is heavily concentrated in the San Francisco Basin and Los Angeles metropolitan areas. Their number—because of the high Mexican birth rate and a steady flow of immigrants—continues to multiply and along with it the overcrowding and slum conditions continue to worsen. *La Raza* will therefore continue to be concentrated in *barrios* of poverty; and Mexicans will increasingly be subjected to dead-end jobs or no jobs at all, bad housing, unhealthy surroundings, fragmented, disrupted communities, and an ever-growing sense of alienation. More than thirty years ago, when society in general was faced with the same problem, it deported Mexican Americans by the thousands back to Mexico. This time, Chicanos may not be so willing to leave their homeland.

Meanwhile, in the *barrios,* a new Chicano has emerged. *Chiques* erupted in rioting in July 1971. Santa Paula, during the first half of 1972, was the scene of several major disturbances. During the 1970–1971 period, East L.A. was the most riotous area in the nation. In each case, rioting was incited by contact with police, but the object of violence in terms of damage and destruction was the central business district, a symbol of the *gringo* establishment within the *barrio*. More and more Chicanos have become aware of their oppression and have struck out angrily against it. After a recent *barrio* riot, one merchant said, "I wish I knew what they wanted but I don't." Perhaps what they want is control of their *barrio*.

II

WHY are Mexicans trapped in *barrios* of poverty? One answer has already been given by rock- and bottle-throwing Chicanos in the streets. Another has been given by Anglo sociologists and social scientists.

Several writers have dominated "Mexican American" studies for the past ten years. The experts include Lyle Saunders who wrote *Cultural Differences and Medical Care: The Case of the Spanish-Speaking People of the Southwest;* Florence Kluckhohn who wrote *Variations of Value Orientations;* William Madsen who wrote *The Mexican Americans of South Texas;* and Celia S. Heller who wrote *Mexican American Youth*. These books are *required* reading for college and university students interested in learning more about the Mexican American people. Without exception, the experts urge upon their readers one dominant theory—cultural determinism. It maintains that the Chicano's negative, fatalistic, and low-aspiration culture has determined his poverty and low status in society; the Mexican's culture does not sufficiently motivate him to succeed in American society. In other words, what's wrong with the Mexican is the fact that he's a *Mexican!* If Mexicans are to succeed in a modern and competitive society, they must be "*gringo*ized" or Angloized in their values and goals. A whole generation of teachers, social workers, clergy, and so on has been taught according to this philosophy of social betterment for the Chicano. This is the ideological genesis of Anglo settlement houses, "cultural enrichment" programs for *barrio* children, and school policies which forbid Chicanos from speaking their own language or being proud of their heritage and customs while in school.

In his study of cultural determinism, Nick C. Vaca, a Fellow at Berkeley's Center for Advanced Mexican American Social Research, listed the following excerpts from Lyle Saunders as an example of the sharp contrast drawn between "negative" Mexican American culture and "positive" American culture and values:

> Unlike the Anglo, the Spanish-American or Mexican-American is likely to be strongly oriented toward the present or the immediate past. He is not a visionary, with his eyes on the golden promise of the future. . . .[9]
>
> There is probably nothing the Anglo more completely accepts than the notion that change is good and progress inevitable. . . . The Spanish-speaking person, coming from another background, has somewhat different orientations toward change and progress. . . . He may distrust and fear the changing future into which the Anglo so buoyantly rushes.[10]
>
> Anglos are doers. . . . Work for them is a value in itself regardless of the return it may bring. . . . Associated with the emphasis on work is the Anglo's preoccupation with success. . . . In attitudes toward work, success, efficiency, and practicality the ideal viewpoint of the Spanish-speaking is *to be* rather than to do.[11]
>
> A closely related trait of the Spanish-speaking people is their somewhat greater readiness toward acceptance and resignation than is characteristic of the Anglo. Where it is a belief of the latter that man has an obligation to struggle against and if possible to master the problems and difficulties that beset him, the Spanish-speaking is more likely to accept and resign himself to whatever destiny brings him.[12]
>
> Among the cherished values of the Anglo is a preference of

independence and a corollary dislike and distrust of the dependent state. . . . In the culture of the Spanish-speaking people independence is not given nearly so high a value.[13]

One observation that is frequently made about the Spanish-speaking people of the Southwest is that the group has been unable to develop effective leadership from among its members or to organize successfully for the purpose of improving its status with respect to the rest of the population. . . . Anglos, as many observers have noted, are great joiners, and their way of meeting a problem is first to set up a committee to study and report on it and then to create an organization to deal with it.[14]

Many Anglos (and even some Mexican Americans) in important and influential positions—teachers, lawyers, community workers, government officials—have read such descriptions and filed them away in their minds as true statements about Mexican people. The cultural determinist theory may not be outright racism since it does not claim that the Mexican is innately inferior; but it does claim that the Mexican, insofar as he is a Mexican, has internalized negative values which cripple his intellectual capacity and inhibit his ability to participate in society. It amounts to the same thing. For those who believe in cultural determinism, the answer to the Mexican "problem" is the eradication of the Mexican's sense of identity.

Other writers like Carey McWilliams and George I. Sanchez have written more realistic and objective accounts of the Mexican people in the United States. Their studies presented the Mexican not as someone hopelessly crippled by negative culture but as victimized by a complex web of racial prejudice and economic discrimination. According to Vaca, the cultural determinist theory prevailed over the interpretations of Sanchez and McWilliams because it was ideologically preferable:

By viewing the causality of the social ills of the Mexican American as stemming from within himself—his cultural baggage—all complicity

> was removed from American society; and thus not only were Southwestern and Midwestern industrial complexes absolved of creating any social ills, but other social institutions . . . were absolved of any complicity.[15]

The thrust of the theory, that Mexicans are inferior because of their values, traditions, culture, et cetera, runs deeply within general society's bias against anything or anyone foreign or colored. It was not difficult for people with such biases to seize upon a particular explanation that emphasized the inferiority of Mexican culture as compared with Anglo culture. It reinforced all that they had been taught to believe: the basic superiority of Anglo-white culture and the deprivation of anyone not in that select category. The flaw in the theory, however, is that the behavior and living patterns of poor Mexican people were identified and made synonymous with the values and culture of all Mexicans. Not only was the theory wrong, but it was also a great insult to the Mexican people, whose hallmark is diversity. A personal experience of mine may help to make this point more clearly. Some years ago, a college classmate, an Anglo from Austin, Texas, was taking a course in sociology and read Madsen's *Mexican Americans of South Texas*. Madsen's description of the Mexicans of South Texas is in the classic tradition of cultural determinism. Among other things, Madsen wrote that "Mexicans believe that God rather than man is controlling events, that is why they lack a future orientation; the Mexican is dedicated to living the moment to its fullest extent in the roles he finds assigned to him by God. . . ."[16]

My friend, whose friendship I have since doubted, told me that Madsen's book helped him to understand me better. I didn't want to get into an argument with him (which would have been futile in any case), so I said nothing at the time. But such a statement, even with the most favorable interpretation given to its meaning, could only be received by Mexican people as the worst kind of insult. Perhaps I should have responded to his remark by saying, "Since we Mexicans are supposed to accept whatever happens to us as from the hands of God, I am happy to accept your demeaning and dehumanizing stereotype of me and the millions of other Mexicans who live in the United States."

No one would deny that Madsen and others actually observed the behavior they reported in their clinical studies. The phenomenon itself is valid, but what is wrong is the absolute interpretation imposed on the data. Certainly, a great many Mexican Americans are content with their lot (especially those who have assimilated as far as the upper middle class!), but is the contentment or resignation to fate that characterizes the poor a value orientation or merely the way *all* poor people, those within the culture of poverty, rationalize and cope with unpleasant unreality? In other words, does the value system as interpreted by Madsen and others lead Mexicans into poverty and keep them there, or are the living conditions of poverty, abject and intolerable poverty, responsible for what is observed as value orientation? Professor Eliu Carranza of San Jose State College believes that *poverty* is responsible for certain attributes which have been wrongly labeled "Mexican American culture."[17]

What has been proposed as the negative value system of all Mexicans, one that teachers and school counselors have frantically tried to root out of Mexican youth, is really nothing more than the attributes of all miserably poor people, whether they be Mexicans, blacks, Irish, Poles, or Italians. A fact too easily forgotten by hyphenated Americans of European descent is that most immigrant groups in this country were once the object of the stereotypes attributed to Chicanos: they drank too much, produced too many children, were prone to violence, were fatalistic, et cetera. Even though the Mexican American is not a true immigrant in the sense that the Irish and others were, the Mexican has been stereotyped and calumniated by false propaganda about "foreigners" longer than any other group.

Striking similarities can be seen between the attributes of the culture of poverty and those of so-called Mexican culture. What Madsen, Saunders, and others saw as uniquely Mexican behavior was actually that of extremely poor people acting as any class of human beings would act under similar pressures. If anything should have been learned from the sociological treatises it is not the finer points of Mexican culture but how miserably *poor* so many Mexican people have become in the midst of affluence.

Mexican values—if we speak of what a people values and seeks to achieve for itself—are not negative. Few Mexicans would accept that judgment of their values. Mexicans are not negative, one-dimensional figures living on the outer limits of the white man's history as they are so often described (whether in books by Ph.D.'s or TV commercials by the Frito Bandito). Mexicans are not pawns who have allowed themselves to be crucified without a struggle. The historical record will bear this out: Mexicans are a living people who have been active in building their own history and who have contributed a long and glorious, albeit unrecognized, chapter to the history of this country.

Perhaps a moratorium should be called on the expert opinions and theories which have been used as explanations of the Mexican's plight. Or if something must be said, it should be as accurate as possible. Since Chicanos are numerically so large and internally so diverse very little can be said by way of generalization. It might accurately be said that (1) most Mexican Americans have come from Mexico or are descended from parents or grandparents who came from Mexico; (2) most speak Spanish and some speak English with an accent; (3) and most have dark coloration—black hair, brown eyes, and brown skin—which makes them, like black people, a visible minority within Anglo-white society.[18] These are the only attributes which can be fairly applied to Mexican Americans as a group; they are the essential characteristics of Chicanos as an ethnic group.

It may also be fairly said that most Mexicans over twenty-five years old have had less than eight years of school; and that between thirty and forty percent of all Mexican families earn less than $3,000 per year, which places them in a culture of poverty. But these facts are nonessentials; they exist not by virtue of the Chicano's character, culture, or ethnic background but by virtue of the kind of society in which Chicanos live. Unfortunately, these nonessentials have been found in the Chicano community for so long that many observers have equated them with Mexican culture.

III

IF MEXICAN CULTURE is not responsible, what accounts for so many Mexicans living in the *barrios* of poverty?

Mexican poverty and degradation are a direct result of American *racism*. In this country, Chicanos have always been viewed as basically inferior to whites. Many white people would vehemently deny this by saying, "America has been good to Mexicans, it has given them fantastic opportunities; they are certainly better off here than in Mexico." And others would protest their personal innocence of racism by saying, "But I'm not a racist; my brother is married to a fine Mexican girl," or "My favorite food is tacos," et cetera.

While they may be truthfully and sincerely expressing their feelings, they fail to understand both the nature of American society and the racism which infects it to the core. The United States long ago ceased to be a tightly knit series of friendly local communities. The most obvious characteristic of this society is that it is a highly complex and sophisticated system of institutions. Individual persons have no influence in society. For instance, an overt bigot is powerless to do any real harm. He is quickly repudiated by most citizens, and often the law forces him to stop bothering persons who are the objects of his prejudice. But when institutions—in their policies, standards, and practices—are biased against Mexicans and other people of color, great power and weight are brought to bear in crushing people. The United States is a racist nation not because its citizens are overt racists (most are not), but because its institutions are geared toward Anglo-white people. The schools are a good example:

> I'm sitting in my history class,
> The instructor commences rapping,
> I'm in my U.S. History class,
> And I'm on the verge of napping.
>
> The Mayflower landed on Plymouth Rock.
> Tell me more! Tell me more!
> Thirteen colonies were settled.
> I've heard it all before.
>
> What did he say?
> Dare I ask him to reiterate?
> Oh why bother.
> It sounded like he said,
> George Washington's my father.
>
> I'm reluctant to believe it,
> I suddenly raise my *mano*.
> If George Washington's my father,
> Why wasn't he Chicano?
>
> —RICHARD OLIVAS[19]

The political party system, employment practices, welfare agencies, police, hospitals, the universities and colleges, are also characterized by institutional racism. In Sturdivant's study, as we saw briefly, certain banks in East Los Angeles refused to lend money to Mexican Americans. These loans are important to people who may want to start a business, repair their home, or avoid long-term indebtedness through the "easy-credit" contracts offered by unscrupulous merchants in the community. Banks that deny such loans say Mexicans can't meet criteria they have established. Obviously Mexicans can't meet the standards, which are oriented toward Anglo-white people in the middle class. Poor Mexicans don't qualify just as they haven't qualified in white society for the past century. And the vicious circle is perpetuated.

Is it any wonder that racist institutions are burned and looted by angry, frustrated *barrio* youths! These institutions embody the worst attitudes of any individual bigot and do infinitely more harm. And while most Americans loudly protest their innocence of racial prejudice and boast of their love of fair play and equal opportunity for all, the fact is that America's institutions can only operate and continue to do harm because of the average citizen's support.

The end result of institutional racism has been the subordination of Mexicans in a culture of poverty with no exit. They are unemployed or subemployed with low skill or no-skill job classifications; and there is no hope of moving up the income scale.

Besides being occupationally segregated, Mexicans were victimized by a change in the economy which accelerated millions of other American workers into better-paying, unionized jobs but left poor Mexicans, poor blacks, and poor whites in a culture of poverty which has been vividly and classically described in Harrington's *The Other America*. Along with millions of other disadvantaged poor people, Mexicans were at the wrong place at the wrong time in the economy when the change came.[20] Often they were in jobs that were unorganizable because of their seasonal nature, or in jobs that were simply overlooked or excluded by the labor movement. Today the lack of education which characterizes such a large percentage of the Mexican population is an insurmountable barrier to better-paying jobs which require at least a high school education or some initial skills.

Agricultural workers, more than any other group in the United States, have been brutally victimized by a society which can advance the super-efficiency of corporate farming while utterly disregarding the human rights of the farm workers. In 1960, nearly half of all Spanish-speaking Americans listed as part of the domestic labor force were agricultural workers. But in ten years, in California alone, the number of farms has been drastically reduced from 135,000 to about 80,000 highly mechanized operations. Mexicans were prime targets for the resulting job displacement. They were the modern-day *enganchados* who were hooked by American institutions that dealt with agriculture management and ownership on a collective basis (and with generous subsidies and other financial incentives) while dealing with hundreds of thousands of farm workers on an individual basis; the popular fiction was that poor *campesinos* had the "right to work" in the fields at the wages offered or the "right" to go elsewhere.

And as hundreds of millions of American tax dollars have gone into mechanizing Southwest agriculture, workers have been put out of the only jobs they know. They continue to drift from Fresno, Sacramento, and Bakersfield on their way to the big *barrios* of Los Angeles and Oakland. When they arrive, they have to start all over again—at the bottom.[21]

IV

"WHY DON'T CHICANOS organize themselves and use their collective power to better conditions in the *barrios?*"

That question has been asked again and again by both Mexican Americans and Anglos who have failed to understand the impact of poverty in the *barrio* as well as the history of Chicanos in the Southwest. It is important to remember that historically Mexicans have been prevented by force from organizing. Although the Mexican American War officially ended in 1848, violence between Anglos and Mexicans continued well into the twentieth century. From 1848 to 1920 there was literally blood all along the border; Vasquez, Cortina, Pancho Daniel, and Pancho Villa were only a few in the long history of Mexican *guerrilleros* who fought the U.S. Army and were never subdued by the Americans. And throughout the region, where strong feelings or hatred existed between the races, Chicanos were physically prevented from organizing. One of the most recent examples was the 1967 attempted suppression of Reies Lopez Tijerina's *Alianza Federal de Mercedes by* New Mexico law officials. Besides the violent tactics of police and other law officials, "extreme economic manipulation" inhibited any involvement of Mexicans in American society.[22]

When some Mexican American organizations started to appear in the 1920s, they were afraid to call themselves "political" lest they provoke the Anglo power structure.[23] Thus the *Orden Hijos de America* and League of Latin American Citizens were founded in Texas to fight discrimination and encourage voter registration while reassuring a distrustful Anglo society that they were loyal Americans committed to working within the system. The Mexican American Political Association (MAPA), Political Association of Spanish Speaking Organizations (PASSO), and G.I. Forum arose in the 1940s and '50s as attempts to politicize *barrio* people and bring about social changes. Chicanos have always attempted to organize themselves despite violent opposition and the threat of deportation; but only within the last fifteen or twenty years has the climate for political organization been favorable.

Today there are hundreds of organizations working to better the lives of *barrio* residents. In East L.A., one of the most important has been the Community Service Organization (CSO) which began in 1947. Its main thrust, inspired by the community action ideas of Saul Alinsky and Fred Ross, was in the political arena. CSO conducted massive voter registration drives and in 1949 was largely responsible for electing Edward Roybal to the city council; Roybal was the last Mexican American to serve on the council. In 1960, CSO joined other *barrio* organizations in registering tens of thousands of *raza* who voted Democratic and helped elect John F. Kennedy President.

The statewide CSO organization also pressured government officials to open up public housing to Chicanos. And it initiated several investigations into police malpractice against Chicanos which resulted in the convictions, suspensions, and dismissals of several police officers. "The main emphasis of

CSO," says Tony Rios, executive director of the East L.A. and statewide organizations, "is organizing grass-roots people, enabling them to deal with social, economic, and political problems now. Until our people find themselves the owners of businesses, we'll never get out of the bag we're in." But to many observers, CSO has largely been a middle-class operation whose conventional working-within-the-system approach is now outdated and unattractive to younger Chicanos. Its membership rolls have dwindled, Alinsky's Industrial Areas Foundation withdrew support, and many important members have left for other organizations. One of CSO's most famous alumni, César Chavez, worked as a statewide organizer for ten years before becoming discouraged with what he felt was CSO's lack of real contact with grass-roots people.[24] So he returned to the fields to organize farm workers.

Perhaps César Chavez should return to East L.A. to organize the urban poor.

"César would run into the same problems I do now," says TELACU's Esteban Torres, who has managed to handle problems pretty well in the four years since The East Los Angeles Community Union (TELACU) was founded. "And César would probably turn a lot of people off who can't relate to his farmworker image or nonviolent style of social change." Torres, a young, college-educated Chicano, may not have a farmworker image, but, in reality, the organization he directs is an urban model for what Chavez did so successfully in rural California. It acts as a power base for *barrio* people attempting to deal with society's institutions. TELACU began in 1968 when trade unionists from the *barrio* came together and sought the assistance of several major unions like the United Auto Workers to help in creating a new organization of *barrio* people, regardless of union affiliation, who would be able to use union strategy and know-how in achieving community control for themselves. Torres, who was born and reared in East L.A., was for many years a UAW International representative to Latin America until Walter Reuther, who took an active interest in the problems of the *barrios,* encouraged him to join in founding the community organization.

"East L.A. is very much like the colonies of Latin America," says Torres. "It is like a small nation that is dependent on foreign markets—the U.S. for one—that keep it in a captive state." As a result of that servitude, the *barrio* remains underdeveloped, without diversity, with no spreading of wealth among *barrio* people. "Of course," adds Torres, "TELACU is only in the formative stages; it will be a long time before the community can be organized to reach a level of real self-determination. But we're working toward that end."

At present, TELACU is trying to establish a strong constituency of dues-paying and share-holding members and thus gradually create community control of local business in the *barrio*. Funded by a variety of public and private grants, TELACU has opened a mattress factory on Brooklyn Avenue and a gas station on Atlantic Boulevard which not only train local people in business management and skills but sell needed products to people within the area. Eventually the factory will be owned by local residents through a stockholding plan which both workers and consumers now participate in. Similar control over the gas station will be passed on to the people. "Whatever TELACU builds," says Torres, "will become part of the people and the community." TELACU is also the first nonprofit organization which has begun to build homes in East L.A. under the sponsorship of the Federal Housing Authority. This was urgently needed because the banks had "red-circled" *barrio* areas as bad risks. The strategy behind TELACU's programs is to overcome some of these barriers and enable the people to own and operate the economic institutions within their neighborhood, to generate jobs and money among Chicanos on a continuing basis.

TELACU is attractive to many young Chicanos who see in the economic base that is being built the beginning of a new nation, Aztlan. Only when this new nation has been built will Chicanos no longer have to ask, hat in hand, for government-sponsored programs, most of which are too little and too late for the vast majority of *barrio* people. *If* there is economic leverage in Aztlan, Chicanos will be able to take their rightful place in society. That is why more power bases like TELACU are so desperately needed now.

NOTES

1. George I. Sanchez, *Forgotten People: A Study of New Mexicans* (Albuquerque: University of New Mexico, 1940), pp. 18ff, 70ff.

2. Leo Grebler, Joan W. Moore, Ralph C. Guzman, *The Mexican-American People: The Nation's Second Largest Minority* (New York: The Free Press, 1970), pp. 250, 252.

3. Lawrence B. Glick, "The Right to Equal Opportunity," in *La Raza: Forgotten Americans,* edited by Julian Samora (Notre Dame: University of Notre Dame Press, 1966), p. 107.

4. Frederick D. Sturdivant, "Business and the Mexican-American Community," *California Management Review* (Vol. XI, No. 3, Spring 1969), pp. 73–80.

5. *Ibid.*, p. 77.

6. *Ibid.*, p. 78.

7. *Ibid.*, p. 77.

8. Ernesto Galarza, "Rural Community Development," *El Grito* (Vol. I, No. 2, Winter 1968) p. 24.

9. Lyle Saunders, *Cultural Differences and Medical Care: The Case of the Spanish-Speaking People of the Southwest* (New York: Russell Sage Foundation, 1954), p. 119. Quoted in Nick C. Vaca's "The Mexican-American in the Social Sciences: Part II: 1936–1970," *El Grito* (Vol. IV, No. 1, Fall 1970), p. 46.

10. Lyle Saunders, *op. cit.*, pp. 123–124.

11. *Ibid.*, pp. 125–127.

12. *Ibid.*, p. 128.

13. *Ibid.*, pp. 133–134.

14. *Ibid.*, pp. 135–136.

15. Nick C. Vaca, *op. cit.*, p. 46.

16. Quoted in Charles B. Brussell's *Disadvantaged Mexican American Children and Early Educational Experience* (Austin, Texas: Southwest Educational Development Corporation, 1968), p. 34.

17. Eliu Carranza, *Pensamientos on Los Chicanos: A Cultural Revolution* (Berkeley: California Book Company, 1969), p. 25.

18. Edward J. Casavantes, *A New Look at the Attributes of the Mexican American* (Albuquerque: Southwestern Cooperative Educational Laboratory, Inc., 1969), Table B.

19. Richard Olivas, "Bronze" 1968 (San Jose *barrio* newspaper), quoted in Octavio Ignacio Romano's "The Historical and Intellectual Presence of Mexican-Americans," *Voices: Readings from El Grito,* edited by Romano (Berkeley: Quinto Sol Publications, Inc., 1971), p. 86.

20. Michael Harrington, *The Other America* (Baltimore: Penguin Books, 1962), p. 13.

21. Ernesto Galarza, Herman Gallegos, Julian Samora, *Mexican-Americans in the Southwest* (Santa Barbara: McNally & Loftin, 1969), p. 8.

22. See Joan Moore's *Mexican Americans* (Englewood Cliffs: Prentice-Hall, Inc., 1970), especially the chapter contributed by Alfredo Cuellar on the political history of *La Raza* in the United States.

23. Joan W. Moore, "Colonialism: The Case of the Mexican Americans," *Social Problems* (Vol. 17, No. 4), Spring 1970, p. 468.

24. Stan Steiner, *La Raza: The Mexican Americans* (New York: Harper & Row, 1969), p. 314.

CHAPTER FIVE

La Educacion de Chicanos

LATE IN 1967, a group of Chicano students at Lincoln High School in East Los Angeles went to Sal Castro, a Chicano teacher, and told him, "We're planning to blow out [walk out or strike]. Will you help us?"[1] They explained to Castro that there were other Chicano students in *barrio* schools who were bitterly dissatisfied with conditions in the schools and felt that the best way to bring about change would be to blow out. Castro advised them to work within the system as much as possible so that if a walkout was necessary, the administration would not be able to criticize the students as unthinking radicals.[2]

"The original plan," said Castro, "was to go before the Board of Education and propose a set of changes, without walking out—to hold that back to get what they wanted. Then, at Wilson High [on] Friday (March 1, 1968) the principal cancelled a play they were going to do ("Barefoot in the Park") as unfit and the Wilson kids blew out. It was spontaneous."[3] The principal's action was typical—arbitrarily done at the last minute, without consultation and without regard for the students who had worked for many months in rehearsing and preparing for the show.[4] Four hundred Wilson students walked out of classes.

Other school administrators would soon regret the Wilson principal's decision, because within 72 hours, several other East L.A. schools, including Lincoln, Garfield, Roosevelt, and a number of neighboring junior high schools in Los Angeles and Montebello, also blew out. Eventually 5,000 kids walked out of their classrooms—they walked out and didn't return. To no one's surprise, police and the district attorney made every effort to crush the uprisings by wholesale arrests and beatings of students on strike lines in front of the schools and the Board of Education. Thirteen strike leaders were indicted on "conspiracy" (a felony) charges. The so-called conspirators, among whom Sal Castro was the best known, were members of a small group of teachers, parents, and other members of the East L.A. community who originally tried to head off precisely such a confrontation by listening to the students' grievances and trying to assist them in airing their views through the proper channels. The charges were later dropped.*

But the most surprising and radical thing about the "Blow Outs" was that when the kids walked out of school, their parents and the entire Chicano community in East L.A. backed them up. Parents who had never attended a PTA meeting and whom Anglo teachers considered apathetic about their children's education, now were walking picket lines with their sons and daughters. Parents jammed into police precincts to protest the arrest of their children.[5] Parents and their striking children went—unannounced and uninvited—to Board of Education meetings to confront school officials with their complaints and demands.

It was, as one reporter wrote, the Mexican American revolution of 1968.[6] Parents, children, and the entire community had joined in the first acts of mass militancy among Chicanos in Southern California.[7]

Why?

I

. . . The Mexican American has [a lower] educational level than either black or Anglo; the highest dropout rate; and the highest illit-

*Castro, who was suspended from teaching duties at Lincoln when indicted, was reinstated in Fall 1968 because of intense community pressure on the Board of Education.

eracy rate. These truths stand as massive indictments against the present educational system. As well, they are indictments of either negligent or intended homicide against a minority group. In essence, what this system has done is to smother the soul and spirit of an entire people.

—MARIO OBLEDO[8]

THE SCHOOL EXPERIENCE has psychologically mutilated the Chicano child. This systematic destruction of human potential has taken place for generations and continues largely unchanged today, despite the protests of the Chicano community. I've already spoken of my own bitter experiences in Los Angeles public schools. Similar but even more severe experiences have been repeated hundreds of thousands of times, as many times as there are Mexican American children who are hopelessly divided between two worlds—school and home.

In the Southwest at least 17 percent of all public school children are Mexican Americans.[9] The figure would be twice as high except for the dropout rates that eliminate nearly 50 percent of all Chicano students. Nine percent of all Chicano students have dropped out by the eighth grade; and 40 percent have dropped out by the twelfth grade.[10] In the predominantly Chicano high schools that "blew out" in March 1968, the dropout figures by the twelfth grade were as follows: Garfield—57 percent; Roosevelt—45 percent; Lincoln—39 percent; Belmont—35 percent; and Wilson—21 percent.[11]

The overwhelming majority of those who remain in school would probably be as well off if they dropped out, too. For most of them fail to achieve even the minimal standards established by the schools. Between 50 and 70 percent of all Chicanos in grades four, eight, and twelve read below average while only 25 to 34 percent of Anglo children on the same grade levels read below average.[12] But it is the schools that have failed, not the children—a failure that reflects the way American society has rejected, mistreated, misunderstood, and disparaged Mexican American people. It amounts to nothing less than genocide of the intellect.

In his study, "Montezuma's Children," Dr. Philip D. Ortego has elaborated in statistical detail how the schools have failed to educate Mexican Americans. Chicanos average 7.1 years of schooling—five years less than Anglos and two years less than blacks.[13] In Texas 39 percent of all Mexican Americans have less than a fifth grade education; those who are twenty-five years of age or older have as little as 4.8 years of formal education. When the entire Mexican American population in Texas is considered, half of them are functional illiterates (1–4 years of school).[14] In Colorado the median average of education for Chicanos fourteen years of age or older was 8.6 years. In New Mexico the figure was 8.4 years, and in Arizona, 7.9 years.[15] California, which offers the *best* educational opportunities to Chicanos, reports a 50 percent dropout rate between the tenth and eleventh grades.[16] In the entire Southwest, 29 percent of all Chicanos fourteen years of age or older are either illiterate or functionally illiterate.

Colleges and universities enroll hundreds of thousands of young students each year, but only two percent of the college population is Mexican American, while only one half of one percent graduate.[17] In New Mexico half the population is Mexican American, but less than eight percent attend the state colleges and university. At the University of Texas in Austin in 1969 I spoke with several embittered young Chicano students who told me that only 300 Chicanos were enrolled out of a total student body of 35,000 (twenty-three percent of Texas' population is Mexican American). In California less than one half of one percent of college students at the seven campuses of the University of California were Chicanos. "We have more enrollees at San Quentin," says Vicente Jimenez, "than in all the colleges of California."

But statistics fail to convey the traumatic dilemma of Mexican American children in school. The child is not only subjected to a repressive curriculum and atmosphere but made to feel ashamed of his ethnic identity and family. "How can a dark-skinned six-year-old love his skin color," asks Uvaldo Palomares, "if he is surrounded by books, children, and adults who value only fair skin?"[18] And how can such a child be proud of himself and his *raza* when not only his skin color but his language, diet, family customs, clothing, and even his natural capacity to learn are disparaged by white Anglo teachers in an Anglo-oriented system?

II

> Although schooling is idealized as the way to rise in the status system, the local society, if it is to be maintained, requires that children be prepared to occupy the particular slots that the community has available for different categories of its population.
>
> —THOMAS P. CARTER[19]

THE PRIMARY REASON why schools have been allowed to twist and destroy the human potential of generations of Chicanos is that the schools accurately reflect American society in all its institutions. Schools and the personnel who staff them are basically conservative. In the Southwest, Mexicans have traditionally filled only certain jobs in much the same way that blacks filled only manual labor and domestic roles (mammies, cooks, servants) in the South.[20] The parallel is a good one. Anywhere one travels in the Southwest, Mexicans can be seen as the ones who fill the lowest positions—in carwash operations, restaurants, shopping centers, and so on. And in the public school system (where only 4 percent of all teachers are Chicanos)[21] 30 percent of all the janitors are Chicanos.[22]

When the Southwest was primarily agricultural, Mexicans filled a great need by supplying a reservoir of cheap labor. Society had a place for Mexicans working in the fields. Because this is what they were destined for, they had—in society's estimation—little need for education. The little need they did have was met by the schools. Purposefully they turned out Mexicans with poor but basic abilities in reading and figuring, just enough to be able to take orders from the *patrón* and do their work.[23] According to society's standards the schools did a good job in preparing Mexicans for a useful role in life.

Society's unequal hierarchy of jobs and income for *certain* groups was just as decisive (and often more so) in determining the way children would do in later life as were the efforts of the best-motivated and inspired teachers, administrators or curricula. One reason why there is such a high dropout rate for Chicanos is that many are realistic enough to know that the school experience is totally irrelevant to their future life, jobs, income, or status. Generally they will make no more money than did their fathers before them. The entire experience is a tragic and vicious circle: the children enter high school knowing the schools are against them, and the schools predict that the incoming students are dull and of low capacity. Again, this vicious circle is an accurate reflection of the dynamic within society itself, in all its institutions. Anglo children often find school as boring or tiresome as their Chicano classmates do, but the white children know they will be rewarded for staying in school. White-collar jobs, good incomes, et cetera await those who finish.[24]

The schools, then, have done the bidding of Anglo-white society. If they have reflected intolerance, discrimination, and pessimism toward Chicanos it is because *gringo* society has treated the Mexican people in the same way, using the schools as a principal source and instrument of repression. How the American people have taken care of Mexican Americans for the past several generations is a grim and tragic indication of the kind of people they are.

III

They say this is the melting pot. I wonder who invented the melting pot. Horrible term! You melt people down, God! It shouldn't be that way. Our country should be a place where the individual is sacred. We have so many different sorts of people. Every man has his own heart. Who gives you the right to cut out a man's heart and put it in a melting pot?

—LUIS VALDEZ[25]

THE STATED GOAL and underlying assumption of public school theory and practice is that Anglo-white culture is superior to everything else; and everything else must be stripped away or boiled down in the melting pot. This philosophy, when applied to indigenous Mexican American children, has the crippling effect of stripping children of their ethnic identity and pride.

From the moment they enter school, the children are forbidden to speak their own language. While nearly fifty percent of all Mexican American first graders do not speak English as well as their Anglo classmates,[26] five out of every ten *barrio* schools have a "No Spanish" rule in the classroom;[27] Texas makes it a *criminal* offense for teachers, administrators, and school officials to speak to the children in their own language.[28] A typical reprimand heard in classrooms and corridors is: "Don't speak Spanish! You live in the United States!" Then the child's name is changed: *María* becomes Mary; *Tomás* becomes Tom and *Roberto* becomes Bob; *Jesús* becomes Jesse. Psychologists say that a young person's name is very near the core of his personality; when a child's name is changed, something essential to a human person is tampered with.[29] (It is seldom done to other bicultural children; Hans and Pierre would probably not have their names changed; nor would the French or German accents of these students be criticized by school teachers and officials. The implication is that Mexican Americans, their names, accents, and everything about them, is inferior.[30]

During their time in school the children are subjected to constant criticism. They are told, "Stop looking like *pachucos*!" and forbidden to wear certain clothes. Dr. Thomas P.

Carter, during his extensive field research in minority schools in California and Texas, quoted a social worker in Texas: "One of the biggest problems I have in my job is to go and ask a father to tell his son to cut his hair in an Angloized way, with the short sideburns and no bush on top, and the father is wearing his hair exactly like the son. About the only thing you can tell him is that, 'Look, we don't like this at school because children don't dress like that, and we don't want the children to look like adults.' This is really stepping on egg shells."[31] This is one instance among many of the school's attempt to crush the pride of an entire people.

In preparation for his book *Mexican Americans in School: A History of Educational Neglect* (1970), Carter interviewed over two hundred and fifty school people working with Chicano children. The ignorance, lack of preparation and training, and overt prejudice he encountered shook his belief in school people and their work.[32] Teachers he interviewed believed that bilingualism was a "Mexican problem," that two languages were detrimental to the child's intellect or teachability. Others criticized the children for the poor, inferior Spanish they spoke. Many educators seem to feel that their students can only speak "Pocho," "Tex Mex," or "Wetback Spanish."[33] In the historical perspective of the schools' constant efforts to eradicate the Spanish language from the Southwest, it is a tribute to the spirit and pride of the Mexican American people that they have resisted and continue to speak their language.

Predictably, most teachers believed that Mexican culture produced lack of motivation or interest. As we have already seen, the culture they were referring to was a rural folk culture studied in remote areas of the Southwest. Yet the teachers generalized from this limited and incomplete knowledge, not realizing that eighty percent of all Mexicans live in cities and that they have always been a diverse people. And teachers believed that this folk culture produced a negative self-image in the children. This misinterprets a common phenomenon. If the Chicano child cringes or crouches, lowers his head or acts dumb, it is not because of his negative self-image but because he has learned to cope with his school-inflicted handicaps of poor reading ability, poor vocabulary, et cetera, by acting dumb when the teacher calls on him.

Because of the books they read and their own personal biases, teachers were almost universally pessimistic about the Mexican American's ability to learn. They saw the Chicano as inferior to the white child; an inferiority which the overt racists attributed to innate stupidity and which the more "open-minded" ones attributed to laziness or apathy as produced by culture. It never occurred to the teachers (and probably still hasn't) that it was their own ignorance, narrow perceptions, and lack of skills that caused the child to fail. They preferred to blame the child and his culture rather than look critically and professionally at themselves and their institutions. Thus, one California junior high school teacher told Carter: "We will keep trying . . . but there is nothing you can do with these kids, they can't discuss, they can't talk, all you can do is give them seat work to keep them busy and keep them under control."[34]

The problem is not one of disadvantaged students but disadvantaged *teachers*.

And while the schools were either launching a frontal attack on negative "Mexican culture" or blaming it for their own failures, the children were presumably being introduced to the American way of life. This way of life, Carter discovered in his field research, amounted to three cardinal values: (a) extreme cleanliness, (b) respect for law and order, and (c) standard white Anglo middle-class morality and manners. At the core was cleanliness, a fact which confirmed what Chicanos and other minority groups have long maintained: Anglo-white values are based on nothing more substantial or solid than soap suds! The other "values" of law and order and morality likewise were nothing more than attitudes of unquestioning acceptance of society's status quo (rather than internalized beliefs and convictions).

IV

Two school systems exist in the Southwest today—one for Mexican American children and other minority groups and one for whites. This has come about through the segregation and isolation of brown and black children in districts and schools.

Mexican American children were segregated in American public schools on a widespread basis until 1947 when the practice was challenged in the courts. As early as 1930 suits were brought against Texas schools, but despite favorable rulings by the courts, Mexican American children continued to be deprived of their rights to equal education. In the following decade a number of lawsuits were brought against Texas school districts as well as districts in Arizona and California. *Hernandez v. Driscoll* (Civ. No. 13840 U.S.D.C. So. Dist., Texas, Jan. 11, 1957) challenged the Texas practice of requiring *all* Mexican children to spend two years in the first grade simply because they were Mexicans.

James De Anda, a Chicano lawyer from Nueces County, Texas, participated as counsel in many of the desegregation cases. "There has never been a statute or law against Mexicans, it was only by custom or interpretation of law* that we were segregated," said De Anda. "Because of this the courts would often rule that Mexicans were 'white' and as such implied that it was impossible for us to be discriminated against. Another problem we found was the pairing of black and brown school districts to get around the Supreme Court decision [1954 *Brown v. Board of Education* which outlawed the segregation of blacks in schools]." This practice was successfully challenged by the landmark 1970 case, *Cisneros v. Corpus Christi Independent School District* (Civ. No. 68-C-95 S.D. Tex., June 4, 1970). Federal District Judge Woodrow Seals held:

*For many years in California, a state statute which provided for separate schools for "Mongolians" and "Indians" was interpreted to include Mexican Americans under the classification of "Indians."[35]

> . . . it is clear to this court that these people for whom we have used the word Mexican-Americans to describe their class, group, or segment of our population, are an identifiable ethnic-minority in the United States, and especially so in the Southwest, in Texas, and in Corpus Christi. This is not surprising; we can notice and identify their physical characteristics, their language, their predominant religion, their distinct culture, and, of course, their Spanish surnames.[36]

The case proved before the law what had been more than obvious to Anglo society for generations: that Mexicans are "brown" and form an identifiable ethnic-racial minority. The court held that Chicanos must be accorded the same protections as blacks under the *Brown* decision outlawing segregation of visible minorities in schools.

Despite various court rulings, however, the practice of segregation continues unchanged to this day. One reason is that housing patterns have remained unchanged. For instance, the Los Angeles public schools are divided by the Santa Monica Mountains; south of the mountains 64 percent of the students are brown and black, while north of the mountains, 85 percent of the students are white.[37] Recently a study was undertaken of the annual (1970–1971) sixth-grade reading scores for Los Angeles' four hundred and thirty-five schools. It was found that when the scores, computed on a national basis, were ranked and arranged by race, a clear pattern emerged: high scoring children were invariably white, attending schools north of the mountains. These children could read well and could also look forward to becoming technicians, teachers, lawyers, and doctors. But the low-scoring children were either brown or black, concentrated in 146 *barrio* or ghetto schools south of the mountains. They had fallen so far behind the national reading norm that if one of the highest-scoring Chicano or black children were to transfer to an Anglo-white school, he would barely qualify to be on the low end of the Anglo-white list.[38]

In Los Angeles, and everywhere else in the Southwest, there are at least two school systems, separate and unequal:

one for whites and another for the visible brown and black minorities.

Even in racially mixed schools, Mexican American children are isolated by means of the tracking system. This system seeks to group children according to their intellectual ability. Those with low I.Q. scores or who are otherwise viewed as slow learners are placed in special classrooms or "tracks." What determines the child's being assigned to a low-ability track deserves special attention because the decision for all practical purposes classifies the child for the rest of his school career. A child is determined to be slow because of his grades, I.Q. testing, recommendations of school counselors, the teacher's evaluation, et cetera. That most of these criteria tend to be inaccurate and, in the case of Chicano children, often totally inappropriate as evaluators of the children has been proven again and again. Two obvious failings that immediately disqualify most of these criteria are: the widespread inability of teachers and other school personnel to speak Spanish and thus communicate with the children, and the equally widespread inability to correctly interpret scholastic achievement and ability from I.Q. measurements which were designed for Anglo middle-class children, not Mexican Americans.[39]

For years Mexican American children have been given I.Q. tests administered in English and oriented toward Anglo-white children. As a result, a large percentage of the children have been categorized as EMR—"educable mentally retarded." This happens regularly because the children's true intelligence is not manifested by such tests. While only 5 percent of Anglo-white children have been classified as EMR (I.Q. of 75 or below) 13 percent of Mexican American children were so classified. Twenty-five percent of Anglo children were classified as slow (I.Q. of 75–90), but 50 percent of all Mexican American children fell into this category. Fifty percent of Anglo children were classified as average or normal (I.Q. of 90–100), but only 25 percent of Mexican American children were in this classification.[40]

In California, 40 percent of all EMR children were Mexican American children. When some Mexican American children were re-tested in Spanish-language tests, reported the California State Department of Education, the results showed that they had clearly been classified below their actual potential and ability. In one case the I.Q. score of a Chicano child jumped as high as 28 points.[41] The most destructive effect of such testing is that it confirms what many teachers and school administrators already believe—that Chicanos are naturally slow and that the schools are fighting a losing battle by trying to educate them. From the time they enter school the children are looked down upon as nonachievers and treated accordingly.

The segregation and isolation of Chicanos in school is not limited, however, to the students. It is total and complete —involving teachers, parents, and the entire Mexican American community.

Chicano teachers are segregated along with the children. Of the extremely small number of Chicano teachers (a little less than 4 percent are Chicanos while 90 percent are Anglos and 6 percent black),[42] half of all Chicanos are sent to predominantly Mexican American schools in poor *barrios,* and one third are sent to schools that are almost if not completely segregated.[43] Many Anglos are sent to *barrio* and ghetto schools as a punishment (a kind of "banishment") because they are the worst schools in the system. Mexican American teachers, however, seem to be assigned there as a matter of course, as if that is where they belong. (Something can be said for having Chicano-run and -dominated schools which would meet the unique educational needs of our people, but under the present system the almost exclusive assignment of Chicano teachers to *barrio* schools is just another symptom of racial segregation.)

During the "Blow Outs" many Anglo teachers and administrators were stunned by so many parents and community people joining their striking children in protesting school policies and practices. They had believed that Chicano parents were not interested in their children's education or were apathetic about it. Actually, parents and the Chicano community have always been *excluded* (along with Spanish language and culture) from school activities. PTA meetings and notices sent home (the primary means of communication between schools and parents) have invariably been in English, not Spanish. According to the U.S. Civil Rights Commission in 1972, only 25 percent of elementary schools and 11 percent of secondary schools with large Chicano enrollments sent notices home in Spanish to the parents.[44] Only 8 percent of elementary schools and 2 percent of secondary schools with large Chicano enrollments used Spanish in conducting PTA meetings.[45] And during the "Blow Outs" one of the demands was for a community advisory board which would open up the schools to some community participation and make school officials in some way accountable to the people. Very few (only one in four) *barrio* districts have advisory boards with parents and other community people participating on them. And boards which are in existence seldom hold meetings.[46]

V

ONE OF THE PRINCIPAL REASONS why Chicano children perform poorly in school is that the teachers are prejudiced against them. Most teachers would deny that, but one does not have to be an overt racist to be filled with prejudicial attitudes which cripple a child's confidence and actual performance in the classroom. According to Paul M. Sheldon's research into teacher attitudes and their relationship to dropout rates, ". . . grades given to Mexican American students in citizenship subjects such as 'work habits' and 'cooperation' were consistently lower than those given to non-Mexicans."[47] In my own school experience, which I've already discussed, the teachers did not accept us for the sole reason that we were Mexicans. They placed little confidence in us; they did not have the same expectations for us as they did for the white children. They did not view us as the social, intellectual, or cultural equals of the white children.

There is a great deal of evidence concerning the ways teachers' views and perceptions affect Mexican American children. In a carefully controlled experiment conducted in South San Francisco schools, as reported by Carter, researchers tested the influence of teacher attitudes by giving the teachers *false* predictions about the ability of their Mexican American students. Selected on a random basis, the children were predicted to be on the verge of "blooming" academically and intellectually. Only the teachers of the children were informed of this so that parental attitudes were not a factor. The results of the experiment clearly demonstrated that the false predictions, which were accepted as valid by the teachers, were self-fulfilling.

The children made substantial gains in their I.Q. scores. It is significant that those children with the most pronounced Mexican appearance (dark coloring, Indian features) made the most startling advances in academic achievement. Apparently the teachers (as the researchers speculated) showed great surprise and then keen interest in the fact that *even* these children could be expected to bloom as bright, intelligent children. And the more the teachers were attentive to the children, looking into their dark faces for some sign of expected brilliance, the more the children actually achieved.[48]

Young, highly impressionable children are likely to respond to what adults call forth from them. Unfortunately most Anglo adults, and teachers in particular, have been negative and pessimistic about the abilities of Mexican American children. And the children have lived up to expectations.

The situation would not be so critical if the battle lines were only drawn between children and teachers. Unfortunately, the teachers are backed up by the entire educational system, which has always excluded Mexican American culture, history, and folklore from the academic curricula. The Anti-Defamation League of *B'nai B'rith,* in a nationwide study of social studies textbooks used in junior and senior high schools, found that there was not even a single textbook that presented a "reasonably complete and undistorted picture of America's many minority groups." It also concluded that the Mexican American had replaced the black as this country's "invisible man."[49] In the Southwest only 4.3 percent of elementary schools and 7.3 percent of secondary schools include Mexican American history in the curriculum.[50] And of the few textbooks that deal with early Southwest history, says Marcos de Leon, founder and past president of the Association of Mexican American Educators, an extremely biased picture is drawn of the *Mexicano* as one who "wandered around in confusion until the Anglo-Saxon, with his superior wisdom and clearer vision, vaulted the Rocky Mountains and brought order out of chaos."[51]

The exclusion of Mexican history and culture dates back to the Mexican War. In the following passage, José Vasconcelos, Mexican philosopher, recounts his experience as a small child in an American elementary school in Eagle Pass, Texas. The year was 1894:

> My first experience at the school in Eagle Pass was bitter. I saw North American and Mexican children seated in front of a teacher whose language I did not understand. In speaking of Mexicans I include many who, though they lived in Texas and though their parents were naturalized citizens, would make common cause with me for reasons of race. And even if they hadn't wanted it that way, it would have been the same, because the yankees so *classify* them [emphasis mine].
>
> . . . when it was said in class that a hundred yankees would put a thousand Mexicans to rout, I would get up to say, "That isn't true." And it irritated me more if, when speaking of Mexican customs along with those of Eskimos, some student would say, "Mexicans are a semi-civilized people." At my house it was said on the contrary, that it was the yankees who were newcomers to culture. I would get up to repeat: "We had a printing press before you did." The teacher would intervene, placating us and saying, "But look at Joe, he is a Mexican, isn't he civilized? Isn't he a gentleman?"[52]

Generations have passed, but nothing has changed. Most of the children, however, are not as well equipped as José Vasconcelos to challenge anti-Mexican propaganda. In 1969, a recent graduate of one of the East Los Angeles high schools that blew out in 1968 reported the same bitter experiences:

> From the time we first begin attending school, we hear about how great and wonderful our United States is, about our democratic American heritage, but little about our splendid and magnificent Mexican heritage and culture. What little we do learn about Mexicans is how they mercilessly slaughtered the brave Texans at the Alamo, but we never hear about the child heroes of Mexico who courageously threw themselves from the heights of Chapultepec rather than allow themselves and their flag to be captured by the attacking Americans.
>
> We look for ourselves in these history books, for something to be proud of for being a Mexican, and all we see in books, magazines, films, and TV shows are stereotypes of a dark, dirty, smelly man with a tequila bottle in one hand, a dripping taco in the other, a sarape wrapped around him, and a big sombrero.
>
> But we are not the dirty, stinking winos that the Anglo world would like to point out as Mexican. We begin to think that maybe we are inferior, that we do not belong in this world, that—as some teachers actually tell students to their faces—we should go back to Mexico and quit causing problems for America.[53]

VI

SOME SAY THAT PROGRESS has been made since the "Blow Outs" of 1968. Those who are optimistic about what has happened point to the school districts where I.Q. tests in English for the Spanish-speaking have been abolished or limited, as well as numerous projects which have been funded by the federal government to help Mexican American children in school. Millions of dollars have been set aside by the Department of Health, Education, and Welfare for the education of the Spanish-speaking. Unfortunately many of those programs have amounted to a great deal of federal paper-shuffling but little substantial benefit for the Mexican American student.

The Federal Bilingual Education Act of 1967 made limited funds available for bilingual education pilot projects, and in 1969 there were 76 programs, 65 of which were for the Spanish-speaking. According to the Office of Education in Washington, bilingual education is the use of two languages as the media of instruction in a program which includes part or all of the regular curriculum as well as the history and culture associated with the mother tongue being used. "A complete program develops and maintains the children's self-esteem and a legitimate pride in both cultures."[54]

Bilingual education is undoubtedly the single most important program of instruction that could be offered to Chicano students. That is why it was made one of the demands during the "Blow Outs": "Bilingual-bicultural education will be compulsory for Mexican Americans in Los Angeles city school system where there is a majority of Mexican American students. This program will be open to all other students on a voluntary basis." The program is the most effective means devised for overturning the present traditional approach of monolingual, monocultural education in the schools. But for all the talk about bilingual education by the government and the schools, only 6.5 percent of the schools in the Southwest have such programs, and only 2.7 percent of the Chicano students—that is only *one out of every forty* who need it—are actually participating in the programs.[55] Moreover, many of the programs that were funded by HEW were not truly bilingual-bicultural because teachers were inadequately trained, untrained, or incapable of really teaching in both media.[56] According to the U.S. Civil Rights Commission in 1972, "bilingual programs have had little impact on the total Mexican American school population."[57]

Another program, highly praised by some educators, is the English as a Second Language course of instruction which tries to teach Chicanos English in much the same way a foreign language is taught to Anglo students. The program is good insofar as it recognizes that half of all Mexican American children who enter first grade cannot speak English as well as their Anglo classmates. And educators like it because it doesn't require much preparation. But it is clearly not as good as bilingual education because ESL programs do not take into account the unique educational needs of Chicanos. While it appears on paper that there are a great many ESL programs (50 percent of *barrio* schools reported having such a program) less than 10 percent of the Chicano students in *barrio* schools were actually being helped by the programs.[58]

It should come as no surprise that the most popular program to help Chicano students—from the Anglo point of view—was the Remedial Reading program. It is popular with teachers and school administrators because it requires absolutely no preparation, no change in the curriculum, and seeks to adjust the child to the school's expectations. A few hours are set aside each week when the children are drilled in reading fundamentals by a teacher or teacher aide. In effect, it says that Chicano students fail to "measure up" because they are "retarded" in language skills and therefore are in need of "remedial" work; this implies that the fault lies with the child for not doing as well as his Anglo classmates. About 10.7 percent of all Mexican American children in Southwest schools are involved in such programs.[59] But results show that Remedial Reading may be more a part of the problem than the solution. The programs are not doing the job because by the fourth grade, 51 percent of Chicanos are six months or more behind the national reading average; by the eighth grade 64 percent are behind; and by the twelfth grade, 63 percent (of those who have somehow survived the 40 percent Chicano dropout rate) are way behind the national average (some twelfth grade Chicanos read on only a ninth grade level).[60]

Most of the programs in operation, therefore, are well-meaning but at best ineffectual. At worst, they are destructive, because their underlying premise is "change the child to fit the school." And with more and more federal and state money going into such unimaginative, unproductive programs, teachers and school officials have a tendency to say, "Look, you Chicanos, we've tried to help you, we've spent our time and money. Let's see you produce!" Thus inadequate programs which are designated for the Spanish-speaking serve to absolve the schools from further effort and critical self-evaluation. For it is the schools which are in dire need of change, not the children.

If the federal government really wanted to help the Mexican American community, they would allocate enough funds to immediately begin training at least 100,000 bilingual-bicultural teachers and educational administrators; help individual states (Texas is the worst offender) to recognize the great needs of their Mexican American citizens and provide bilingual education programs for them; agitate with federal muscle within state legislatures and governments to give priority to Mexican American affairs where Mexican Americans reside in large numbers.[61]

Radical changes have to be made, changes which will completely eliminate the monolingual, monocultural, Anglo-white triumphalism which characterizes present-day practices and policies. It must be replaced with a more democratically oriented policy—a *cultural democracy* which honors Mexican-brown culture (properly understood and appreciated), language, and values. Spanish-speaking children must be given the opportunity to choose between two cultures or to choose both at once. The premise of cultural democracy, then, is that every culture has value and worth. Every person, white or brown, has value and can contribute something to American society. He doesn't have to first be stripped of his personality, name, language, and ethnic pride before being acceptable in this society as a worthwhile human being. Assimilation must not be absorption but a mutual give and take. If properly educated, the Mexican American can be comfortable in two cultures at once; if properly educated, Anglo-whites will be enriched by the strength and wisdom that Mexican American culture and values have to offer them.

VII

Maybe we should close down our schools for a while and retrain our teachers . . . even if the children were on the streets they'd be learning more than from some of our teachers.

—NEIL V. SULLIVAN[62]

DR. NEIL V. SULLIVAN, one of the nation's foremost educators, may have the best solution to the school problems besetting Chicanos: close down the public schools because they have ceased to be places of learning and have become schools of oppression. But American society and schoolteachers and officials in particular (who make their living from the tax dollars supporting this oppression) are not about to do that, which illustrates the problem. The fault of Mexican Americans failing in school lies with the kind of society we live in and the kind of school society has bred.

No one is going to close down the schools, but Anglo teachers can at least be retrained. And one of the most effective teacher retraining centers in the nation is being conducted in East L.A. as a direct result of the 1968 "Blow Outs."

The Hispanic Urban Center, formerly the El Salvador Baptist Church before it was renovated to serve as a spacious "school" building, is located in one of the most poverty-stricken sections in East L.A. And for the first time in their lives, many Anglo teachers are reporting to this *barrio* center (and not white colleges and universities in suburbia) for their continuing education in such specialized courses as "History of the Mexican American," "Teaching Reading to Bilingual Students," "The Mexican Adolescent," et cetera. The course instructors are all Chicanos, and local residents—parents of Chicano students in East L.A.—are in charge of taking the teachers on field trips into the *barrio,* introducing them to the neighborhoods where their students live.

The In-Service Teacher Training Program, as it is formally called, was first suggested to the L.A. City School

System by the Mexican American Education Commission (MAEC), which was established as the school system's response to the community's demand for greater Chicano involvement in the running of *barrio* schools. (Although MAEC is often criticized by Chicano activists as being a "creature" of the L.A. Board of Education, it was only created over stiff opposition by conservative board members and school bureaucrats because tremendous community pressure was brought to bear during the "Blow Outs.") MAEC told the Board that the purpose of the In-Service Teacher Training Program would be to teach the teachers about their Spanish-speaking students. Sensing another possible confrontation, the School Board reluctantly agreed to the proposal.

In the Spring of 1972, 160 teachers and 80 teacher aides were enrolled; in the Fall, 350 teachers were enrolled in the Center's programs. At this writing, 600 teachers were expected to enroll in the Spring of 1973. Funds for operating expenses came from the American Baptist Convention (which provided the building) and a grant of federal money under the Model Cities Program. Approval and encouragement for teachers to enroll came from the L.A. City School District. The various courses offered through the Center are accredited through Occidental College in Los Angeles, which was even more of an incentive for teachers to participate. What the Center has done in the last year and proposes to continue doing on an ever-growing basis is the first such large-scale effort at "de briefing" or "de-colonizing" the minds of Anglo teachers who work in *barrio* schools. The teachers in the program not only become aware of the needs of Chicano students but also are made to confront their own personal biases toward Mexican Americans. They are asked to look within themselves to answer: "In what ways do I diminish the Mexican American's self-image? How do I reinforce or bring about low motivation or lack of interest among the students? Why should I or anyone else force the child to assimilate?"[63]

"I believe our program has caused some perceptions of Anglo teachers to change and they now have more respect for our children," says Vahac Mardirosian, a Mexico-born Baptist minister of Armenian parents, who directs the Hispanic Urban Center and serves as chairman of MAEC. "Our basic assumption is that expectations rise when respect for a group rises, and respect for Chicanos rises if knowledge about the Chicano people is imparted to teachers in *barrio* schools." Tony Ortiz, one of the Center's full-time instructors, adds, "We can't really change their [the teachers'] attitudes, they're too deeply ingrained; but I think we changed some behavior patterns. Intellectually they can at least see that what they've been doing has been all wrong. We're hoping that because of what they now know they'll behave differently in the future."

How much of a breakthrough does the Teacher Training program represent? "We've taken a turn in a new direction," says Mardirosian. "But our program is only a drop in the bucket. We have a long way to go before we have schools where our children will feel secure and worthwhile—not second-class, as they are now made to feel—and where they can get down to the business of learning—learning in a grand style!"

In 1968, the Chicano community rose up against the schools to protest the inferior education of Chicano children; the dropout rates (that yearly produce 10,000 Chicano dropouts in Los Angeles county alone!); the "mental maiming" (as Dr. Francisco Bravo has said) of Chicano children by unskilled, prejudiced teachers, principals, administrators, and school board members; a monocultural, monolingual curriculum that is an affront to and a violation of, the Treaty of Guadalupe-Hidalgo; and the segregation and isolation of Chicanos and blacks within the worst districts and schools in the system.

Some progress has been made since 1968 even though it is, as Vahac Mardirosian says, "a drop in the bucket." But whatever progress has come about has resulted from Chicanos' becoming realistically aware that Anglo-white society and their schools do not accept us as equals and that we must fight for everything our people need. Without that understanding, the few gains that have been made will be lost, and progress in the future will be impossible. The kids who walked out and the community that backed them up knew this truth. Many more of us have come to realize it as well.

The kids taught the rest of us that gains to be made in education or any other area may have to be made by Chicanos on the streets risking their own personal safety and lives by strongly, and if need be violently, confronting the institutions and people who have been crushing us for generations.

"Work within the system," many tell us. "Perhaps this country will change; maybe a massive conversion will take place to bring Americans to their senses." At one time many of us believed that, but now we see it as nothing more than wishful, counterproductive thinking. Besides, our people don't have time to wait.

"If we were starting tomorrow to right all the educational wrongs being committed against Chicanos," says Vicente Jimenez, "it would take twenty years to complete the job."[64]

And Anglo-white society is not starting tomorrow.

NOTES

1. Dial Torgerson, "'Brown Power' Unity Seen Behind School Disorders," *Los Angeles Times* (Sec. C, p. 1), March 17, 1968.
2. *Ibid.*
3. *Ibid.*
4. F. K. Heussenstamm, "Student Strikes in the East Los Angeles High Schools," *School and Society* (Vol. 100, No. 2340), March 1972, pp. 182–185.
5. Torgerson, *op. cit.*
6. *Ibid.*
7. *Ibid.*
8. Mario Obledo, Hearings before the Select Committee on Equal Education Opportunity of the U.S. Senate, Part 4: *Mexican American Education* (Washington, D.C., August 1970), p. 2519. Quoted in U.S. Civil Rights Commission, *Mexican American Education Study, Report II: The Unfinished Education* (Washington, D.C., October 1971), pp. 8–9.

9. U.S. Civil Rights Commission, *Mexican American Education Study, Report I: Ethnic Isolation of Mexican Americans in the Public Schools of the Southwest* (Washington, D.C., April 1971), p. 17.

10. *The Unfinished Education,* p. 10.

11. Heussenstamm, *op. cit.*

12. *The Unfinished Education,* p. 24.

13. Philip D. Ortego, "Montezuma's Children," *The Center Magazine* (Vol. III, No. 6, November–December 1970). Also see Ortego's "Schools for Mexican Americans: Between Two Cultures," *Saturday Review* (April 17, 1971), p. 63.

14. Ortego, "Schools for Mexican Americans," pp. 63–64.

15. Charles B. Brussell, *Disadvantaged Mexican American Children and Early Educational Experience* (Austin, Texas: Southwest Educational Development Corporation, 1968), p. 22.

16. Ortego, "Schools for Mexican Americans," p. 63.

17. ———, "Montezuma's Children."

18. Uvaldo H. Palomares, "Communication Begins with Attitude," *The National Elementary School Principal* (Vol. I, No. 2, November 1970), p. 47.

19. Thomas P. Carter, *Mexican Americans in School: A History of Educational Neglect* (New York: College Entrance Examination Board, 1970), pp. 14–15.

20. Philip D. Ortego, "Mexican-Dixon Line," *Voices: Readings from El Grito* (Berkeley: Quinto Sol Publications, Inc., 1971), pp. 115–119.

21. *Ethnic Isolation of Mexican Americans,* p. 41.

22. *Ibid.,* p. 48.

23. Carter, *op. cit.,* p. 204.

24. *Ibid.,* pp. 203 ff.

25. Luis Valdez, quoted in Stan Steiner's *La Razo: The Mexican Americans* (New York: Harper and Row, 1970), p. 337.

26. U.S. Civil Rights Commission, *Mexican American Education Study, Report III: The Excluded Student, Educational Practices Affecting Mexican Americans in the Southwest* (Washington, D.C., May 1972), p. 14.

27. *The Excluded Student,* p. 18.

28. *Ibid.,* p. 15.

29. Carter, *op. cit.,* p. 101.

30. *Ibid.*

31. *Ibid.*, pp. 100–101.

32. *Ibid.*, p. 5.

33. *The Excluded Student*, p. 15.

34. Carter, *op. cit.*, p. 14.

35. Guadalupe Salinas, "Mexican-Americans and the Desegregation of Schools in the Southwest," *Houston Law Review* (Vol. 8, 1971), p. 940.

36. *Cisneros v. Corpus Christi Independent School District* (Civ. No. 68-C-95, S.D. Texas, June 4, 1970), pp. 10–11 of unpublished court transcript.

37. Editorial, "The Courts and the Schools," *Los Angeles Times* (Part II, p. 6), June 9, 1972.

38. *Los Angeles Times* (Part I, p. 3), July 5, 1971.

39. Thomas P. Carter, "Preparing Teachers for Mexican-American Children" in *Educating the Mexican American* (Valley Forge: Judson Press, 1970), edited by Henry Sioux Johnson and William J. Hernandez-M., p. 202.

40. Ortego, "Montezuma's Children."

41. *Los Angeles Times* (Part I, p. 1), May 9, 1969.

42. *Ethnic Isolation of Mexican Americans*, p. 41.

43. *Ibid.*, p. 44.

44. *The Excluded Student*, p. 39.

45. *Ibid.*, p. 40.

46. *Ibid.*, p. 43.

47. Paul M. Sheldon, "Mexican Americans in Urban Public Schools: An Exploration of the Dropout Problem," *California Journal of Educational Research* (Vol. XII, No. 1), January 1961, pp. 21–26, quoted in *The Unfinished Education*, p. 40.

48. Carter, *Mexican Americans in School: A History of Educational Neglect*, pp. 114 ff.

49. *The Excluded Student*, p. 31.

50. *Ibid.*

51. *Ibid.*

52. José Vasconcelos, *Ulises Criollo* (Mexico: Ediciones Botas, 1937), translated and quoted by Francisco Armando Rios, "The Mexican in Fact, Fiction, and Folklore," *Voices: Readings from El Grito*, pp. 71 ff.

53. Statement of Rosalinda Mendez, quoted in Charles A. Ericksen's "Uprising in the Barrios," *Educating the Mexican American*, p. 60.

54. *The Excluded Student*, p. 21.

55. *Ibid.*, p. 22.

56. *Ibid.*, p. 24.

57. *Ibid.*

58. *Ibid.*, p. 26.

59. *Ibid.*, p. 28.

60. *The Unfinished Education*, p. 24.

61. Testimony of Senator Jacob K. Javits (R.-N.Y.) before the Senate Appropriations Subcommittee on Educational Appropriations, Tuesday, May 11, 1971.

62. Neil V. Sullivan's statement was quoted in Carter, *Mexican Americans in School: A History of Educational Neglect*, p. 218.

63. Eliu Carranza, *Pensamientos on Los Chicanos: A Cultural Revolution* (Berkeley: California Book Co., Ltd., 1969), p. 9.

64. Vicente Jiménez's statement was delivered in a speech at Harvard University Law School on March 26, 1971.

CHAPTER SIX

Strangers in Our Own Land

MEXICAN AMERICANS have lived as strangers in their own land because justice has been denied them for generations. Millions of Mexicans have lived and worked in this country knowing that they had no equal standing before the law. Mexico honored the Treaty of Guadalupe-Hidalgo by giving up half her territory; the United States has flagrantly violated the same treaty by failing to safeguard and protect the rights of Mexicans in the United States. As we shall see, the history of Mexicans in the United States is studded with continuous violations of their basic human rights. Even as these words are written, the "Chicano Liberation Front" has received public attention in Los Angeles by taking credit for twenty-eight bombings of various public institutions (L.A. City Hall, schools, post offices, banks, and police facilities). These violent actions were taken in the name of "outraged *barrio* communities that are powerless and without rights."[1]

Most people do not condone such violent actions, but when there is no justice what is the alternative? Should widespread illegal and unconstitutional violence by police and other law officials be condoned? Lawlessness exists in the *barrios* and elsewhere because Chicanos have nothing to lose—no political ideology or loyalty to working within the system. Justice, the most important word in race relations, is translated as "*gringo*" in the *barrios*. Brown Beret leader David Sanchez puts it another way: "To Anglos, Justice means 'just us.'" Today those words seem truer than ever before.

I

ON WHITTIER BOULEVARD in the heart of the East Los Angeles *barrio* is the Silver Dollar tavern. Like most taverns and bars along the Whittier Boulevard strip—sometimes called the "Chicano downtown"—the Silver Dollar is exclusively patronized by Chicanos. Tight-mouthed young men play at the pool tables, occasionally exchanging comments with their companions. Older men sit at tables or at the bar. They appear more talkative as they quietly converse with one another or with the barmaid. The juke box blares away in Spanish, usually a Mariachi group singing about unfaithful wives or lovers.

The Silver Dollar is much like all the other bars in the district except for one thing: an ominous-looking gas mask hangs from the wall over the cash register and blankly stares out at all the customers as a grim reminder of a far greater tragedy than the Mariachis sing about. Attached to the mask is a handprinted sign which reads: "In memory of August 29, 1970." That date is vividly inscribed in the memory of every Mexican in the Southwest. It marks the killing of Ruben Salazar—a killing which has become the prime symbol of all the unredeemed injustice and suffering Mexicans have experienced at the hands of police and the Anglo system of so-called justice.

The last time I saw Ruben Salazar alive was in his Hollywood office three weeks before he was killed. He had recently assumed the position of news director for KMEX-TV, the Spanish-language station which reaches over a million Chicano viewers in the Los Angeles metropolitan area. He had wrestled with the painful decision of leaving his job as a reporter for the *Los Angeles Times,* a job he liked very much. After much soul-searching he had accepted the new job because he would be in a better position to serve the Chicano community directly. As news director at KMEX he planned to offer Spanish-language news programs directed toward educating the people politically and culturally, reinforcing self-awareness and pride in *La Raza,* and providing in-depth coverage of *barrio* problems.

Ruben Salazar believed that with such news coverage and analysis, the Chicano community would be strengthened and in a better position to participate in resolving *barrio* problems. On the national level he had been one of the leading figures in the formation of the Chicano Media Council (National Urban Coalition) and had been elected its first chairman. Ruben's face seemed to light up as he told me of his plans for the Fall. He had agreed to teach a course in Berkeley once a week—a course on how Chicanos should best use the media to build up the Chicano community and at the same time present a more realistic image to Anglo society.

That morning in his office, we also discussed the Chicano movement in the Southwest. He was delighted at César Chavez's recent victory in Delano. He also spoke favorably of José Angel Gutiérrez of Texas and Ricardo Romo of California. Gutiérrez had organized the *Raza Unida* party in Crystal City, Texas, which had succeeded in winning every seat of government up for election. Gutiérrez had demonstrated that when Chicanos are organized in those areas where they are the majority they can achieve great gains within the system. Romo had just been chosen as gubernatorial candidate for the Peace and Freedom Party; he had been nominated by the Chicano Political Association. "Romo doesn't really stand a chance," Salazar told me. "But you know, he's the first Mexican American to be on the November ballot in the history of California under the American flag. So it's our way of saying to the Democratic party and to the whole system that we're sick and tired of being shown such little recognition for the past one hundred and twenty years."

When I asked him to assess the significance of Chavez's recent victory, he said, "You know, I covered that strike for the *Times* from the very beginning. At first I thought Chavez didn't stand a chance. The odds seemed impossibly high. But he organized on a broad-based appeal and nonviolently resisted every attempt to make him compromise. He demonstrated that the best approach is still 'Power through unity.' César is our only *real* leader." He was deeply impressed with Chavez's *Christian* approach of nonviolence, and when I asked him what he thought of Corky Gonzalez and Reies Tijerina in New Mexico, he said, "They rant and rave and threaten to burn the establishment down. That's good because most people won't listen unless you rant and rave. But this provides the community with little more than emotional uplift; nothing palpable."

Salazar was a political "moderate"—a reasonable man who believed the Chicanos' grievances could be settled *within* the system. In that sense, our philosophies were much the same at that time, and as we parted we agreed to keep in touch with one another. As I left Los Angeles, I felt great pride and confidence in knowing that such a man was covering the Chicano scene—an excellent journalist and newsman dedicated to serving the best interests of his own people through the media. His tragic death a few weeks later shocked me in a profoundly personal way and was a terrible, bitter blow to the entire Chicano community. All of us had lost a good friend.

On August 29, 1970, Salazar and a news team from KMEX were on hand to cover the National Chicano Anti-War Moratorium demonstration in East Los Angeles. Thousands of Chicanos marched that day along Whittier Boulevard to protest the Vietnam War and emphasize the added injustice of Chicanos' being killed at a two-to-one ratio to Anglos in Indochina. César Chavez and Corky Gonzalez, among others, were scheduled to address the rally, but they never reached the speakers' platform. The rally was over before it really began when police and sheriff's deputies overreacted to minor scuffling on the edge of the crowd and used it as an excuse for charging into the assembly of over 20,000, teargassing and clubbing the people.

This led to full-scale rioting which quickly spread throughout the area. (Later, after the burning rubble was cleared, property damage exceeded one million dollars.)

Hours after the rioting broke out, Salazar and several companions from KMEX stopped at the Silver Dollar just as arson and looting reached a peak in that area. Sheriff's deputies received a report—which later was proved false—that armed men were inside the tavern. The deputies acted quickly—too quickly. Deputy Thomas Wilson approached the building and—although no one in the bar heard any warnings (as they testified later)—fired a tear-gas projectile through the curtained front doorway leading into the tavern. The ten-inch projectile Wilson fired was designated—in large lettering on the shell's casing—for use against "barricaded criminals." It was powerful enough to pierce walls and accurate up to one hundred yards. The missile passed through Salazar's head as he sat innocently on a stool within ten or fifteen feet of the doorway. "It was the wrong weapon at the wrong place at the wrong time," editorialized the *Los Angeles Times*.[2] Clearly Wilson had killed Salazar with unjustified deadly force.

While the entire Los Angeles community was stunned and grief-stricken, Chicanos in the *barrios* began to protest that Salazar had been murdered by the Sheriff's Department. Police wanted him out of the way, it was claimed, because many of his factual, pointed articles in the *Times* on police-community relations were often strong indictments of unjust police practices in the *barrio*. And when Salazar criticized police he was not dismissed as a militant loudmouth but listened to as a professional journalist who had won the respect of both Anglos and Chicanos by his work as a foreign correspondent in Mexico City, the Dominican Republic, and Vietnam. In my opinion, it is unlikely that Salazar was murdered, but all the events that led up to his killing as well as the inquest which soon followed indicated some form of foul play which the police wanted to cover up.

Prophetically, Salazar had written before his death: "There is much bitterness in our Mexican American communities, an ever-increasing bitterness against school systems that psychologically mutilate the Chicano child, against certain police who habitually harass our brown brothers, against local and federal governments that apparently respond only to violence." His own death and the reaction of Chicanos to the tragedy were to transform that latent bitterness to widespread frustration and anger, and escalate the violence to a series of major urban riots in East Los Angeles and throughout the Southwest.

The sixteen-day coroner's inquest was held in the Fall of 1970. It was a major drama set in the context of "ever-increasing bitterness" against repression and injustice.* The inquest was not a formal trial to determine guilt but an investigation into the events of August 29 to ascertain whether or not grounds for criminal prosecution existed. It received massive newspaper and television coverage; the Coroner's Office gave permission for the inquest to be televised live each day, and all seven TV stations in Los Angeles carried it. Unfortunately the inquest did not probe the underlying reasons for burning and looting, which were manifestations of the Chicano community's grievances and alienation; only in a distorted and biased way were the events which led to Salazar's death presented to millions of viewers.

For instance, Raul Ruiz, an editor of *La Raza* magazine, had photographed many scenes that, according to his interpretation, showed police brutality and overreaction. His entire testimony was closely, minutely examined and implicitly rejected. It was pointed out that the bottles in Ruiz's photos were probably "evidence" that Chicanos had been drinking and that strong police measures (what Ruiz had called "overreaction") were warranted. In contrast, the sheriff's cameraman who showed a videotape of Chicanos throwing rocks and bottles was questioned only briefly and not challenged at all. Another example of the one-sided approach was the seating of the deputy district attorney. He sat at the same table with two homicide detectives and was seen in

*I am indebted to *Los Angeles Times* writers Paul Houston and Dave Smith for the following account of the Salazar inquest.

constant consultation with them during the inquest. This was a questionable conflict of interest because it is only from the District Attorney's Office that any criminal prosecution could be brought against the Sheriff's Department. According to the *Los Angeles Times,* "It looked as though three California State agencies—District Attorney's Office, Coroner's Office, and Sheriff's Department—were working to portray Chicanos as the kind of people in great need of policing and who would use guerrilla warfare tactics against innocent deputies which would require heavy police response."[3]

This one-sided approach infuriated many Chicanos within reading or viewing distance of the inquest. One Mexican American woman who had been present at the rally and was later gassed as police intervened, saw the first sessions on television and volunteered her testimony to authorities because she believed that her experience of the rally was much different from that given by police testimony. Mrs. Cora Barba, the witness, angrily and tearfully told the inquest jurors:

> I don't want people to be blaming my people. Everybody blames all Chicanos. And I'm proud to be a Chicana. I will always be a Chicana and if I have to die being a Chicana, I'm going to die being a Chicana! And I don't want them [i.e., police witnesses] talking about my people that way.

Frustration and anger were now at an all-time high in the Chicano community. At the September 29 inquest session—one month after he killed Salazar—Deputy Thomas Wilson was called to the stand. After he had taken the oath as a witness he was asked what he was aiming at when he fired into the Silver Dollar tavern on August 29. Before he could answer, Chicano lawyer Oscar Z. Acosta who was not acting as counsel for either side but had attended all the sessions sitting in the audience, jumped to his feet and shouted: "He was aiming at Ruben Salazar, that's what he was aiming at! This is an obscenity. . . . We are sick of it. This room is polluted with perjury and you know it!" Acosta then led a walkout of about twenty-five Chicano militants and announced that he would boycott the rest of the sessions. Resuming his testimony, Wilson said he had been aiming at the ceiling.

A crucial issue during the inquest was whether Wilson was acting within the limits of his orders and the department's training when he shot the projectile that killed Salazar. The attorney for the Salazar family requested that, to clarify the matter, the sheriff's training manual for use of tear-gas equipment be presented as evidence. Inquest hearing officials refused to subpoena the manual; the Sheriff of Los Angeles County refused to hand it over voluntarily. This refusal to hand over evidence essential to determining whether criminal negligence was involved was what occasioned grave doubts about the inquest's impartiality. It looked like a coverup. The *Los Angeles Times* editorialized: "As long as [the Los Angeles County Sheriff] conceals his department's procedures, public doubts will persist. As long as he evades his obligation to assume responsibility and talk to the people in candor, suspicion will persist."[4] But Sheriff Peter Pitchess refused to hand over the evidence.

The majority verdict of the seven-member inquest jury was that the death of Salazar had come "at the hands of another person." The jurors told *Times* reporters Paul Houston and Dave Smith that they meant to indicate that Wilson's conduct had been negligent. But the District Attorney's Office was quick to state that whatever negligence there may have been was not "criminal." The Sheriff's Department also issued a statement: "There was absolutely no misconduct on the part of deputies involved or the procedures they followed." No official action was taken by either the U.S. Civil Rights Commission or the Justice Department. The Mexican American people were told to take the Police Department's word that no foul play had taken place. Thus, in the *barrios* and other Los Angeles ghettos where Chicanos live, the point was made insultingly clear (in televised color) that there is no justice for the Chicano either in the streets or in the courtroom. This is where the matter officially ended; but in the *barrios,* suspicion, anger, alienation, and outrage prevailed.

A year later, in the Summer of 1971, the uneasiness, frustration, and anger over justice denied were again inflamed as four California law officers (three from Los Angeles and one from San Leandro) were acquitted of alleged civil rights violations in the "mistake" killings of two Mexican nationals.

The policemen, members of a "raiding party," had responded to a report they received—later proved false, as in the case of Salazar's killing—that an armed and dangerous gunman was hiding in a downtown Los Angeles hotel room. The police, without warning or identifying themselves as police (according to testimony of survivors) broke into the hotel room, firing with shotguns and revolvers at the first persons they saw. The unarmed Mexican nationals, who were in shorts and T-shirts preparing to retire for the night, were caught completely by surprise. Two of the men were killed by police fire while the others were injured or wounded.

The police later acknowledged the killings as a "tragic mistake." But when the Justice Department* brought indictments against the officers, an obvious rebuke to local law officials who cleared the policemen of any wrongdoing, top-ranking law and government officials in Los Angeles repudi-

*U.S. Attorney Robert L. Meyer, who was responsible for the grand jury indictments against the four policemen involved in the killing of the Mexican nationals, was forced to resign because the move angered both Police Chief Edward Davis and Sheriff Peter Pitchess, who, in turn, used their political leverage in Washington against Meyer. Meyer's vigorous enforcement of the civil rights of Chicanos was only the last in a series which had angered the local power structure: he had assigned neutral observers from the U.S. Civil Rights Division to cover most of the protest rallies at which either policemen or sheriff's deputies had been on duty; had convened grand juries to hear evidence of alleged police misconduct and civil rights violations; and he had even gone so far as to suggest a grand jury investigation of Salazar's death! (*Los Angeles Times,* January 19, 1972, Pt. I, p. 3).

ated the action as a "federal persecution of local police." Chief of Police Edward Davis said: This is "harassment of police by federal authorities which encourages people like the Chicano Moratorium Committee, Brown Berets, the Black Panther Party, and any Marxist organization. Why, it encourages them to perform." Such vocal and bitter criticisms by the Chief of Police (as well as Sheriff Peter Pitchess and Mayor Sam Yorty) gave many the impression that police not only felt they were above the law (and should not be called into question or challenged in court), but that they had absolutely no regard for the human rights of Mexicans.

The acquittal verdict, then, was seen by Chicanos as an acquittal of police practices. To no one's surprise, rioting broke out in East Los Angeles after the verdict was made public. About one thousand *vatos locos* and sheriff's deputies battled each other in the streets of the *barrios*.[5] It was as if the Chicanos had nothing to lose but their blind and violent fury at an unjust and unresponsive system of law. That riot is possibly the best summary available of current police-community relations in Los Angeles and many parts of the Southwest.

II

MEXICAN AMERICANS have been denied equal justice for so many generations that fear, suspicion, alienation, and hostility have become a way of life. The Chicano knows instinctively that he is not equal before the law—either in the *barrios,* when he is stopped for suspicion of drunk driving, or in the courts, when he stands before a white judge and jury. Whenever the Chicano issues a complaint (perhaps his last act of faith in the system), his complaint goes unheard, his grievance unanswered. And in cities such as Los Angeles, tough police departments have increasingly received the support and approval of most citizens as they escalate their intensive and brutalizing treatment of Chicano "criminals" and "hoodlum militants."

Today millions of Americans have come to experience the Chicano's alienation and sense of powerlessness as they view a governmental and political system filled with hypocrisy, corruption, and deadly injustice at home and abroad. As dissent and efforts by young people to change the system are met by repression, many white Americans are coming to conclusions which have long been the Chicano's gut-level reaction to life in *gringo* society. It has been that way for generations.

Suspicion and distrust of law and government are in the Mexican's blood. The Mexican people came into being as enslaved, oppressed people because of the Spaniard's greed, lust, and deceit. Mexicans lived under this tyranny for more than three centuries. Even after the successful revolution of 1810, Mexico was cursed with a series of dictators and tyrants, from Santa Ana to Porfirio Díaz. They did little to build respect for the institutions of law and justice. Most Mexicans, like the peasant revolutionary leader Emiliano Zapata, knew that if justice were to be obtained, it would be through their own efforts: "Seek justice from a tyrannical government, not with your hat in your hand, but with a rifle in your fist."

And Mexicans along with the American Indians are the only people who were defeated in battle and annexed by the United States. This conquest, motivated by "Manifest Destiny" and maintained by racial prejudice and discrimination, determined how Mexican Americans would perceive American institutions of law—the institutional arms of what often seemed like a hostile, anti-Mexican government. After invading armies defeated Mexican inhabitants (they were not soldiers but ordinary Mexican citizens defending their land and possessions) in battle, they were systematically dispossessed and kept in that inferior status without recourse to law. In New Mexico, as Reies Lopez Tijerina has said, "They stole our land and gave us powdered milk!" The Santa Fe Ring, a group of unscrupulous Anglo lawyers, bankers, and businessmen, gained control of the land and dominated the political scene. For instance, lawyer Thomas B. Coltron acquired 593,000 acres of New Mexico land by "patenting" it in his own name at the Land Office and bribing a few officials. Today those who rightfully and legally own the land have been reduced to abject poverty and the "powdered milk" of welfare aid. In Texas, Arizona, and Colorado, the same pattern emerged and was reinforced by violence, often from law enforcement and government officials.

Within a few short years of the conquest, Mexicans were feeling the effects of the double standard of justice. From 1850 to 1856 in California, according to the people who suffered these injustices, they were kept out of the gold mines as "foreigners," prosecuted for hundreds of crimes, and victimized unjustly by vigilante lynchings. And during the entire period not one Anglo criminal had been prosecuted.[6] Often they took matters into their own hands in an effort to see justice done. Mexicans throughout the Southwest had been guaranteed full and equal status under the Constitution, according to the Treaty of Guadalupe-Hidalgo; but the rights, liberties, and equal status were never provided or protected by the American system of justice.

Mexicans were regarded by whites as inferiors who were characterized by the basest of human qualities. From the time of the Alamo, they were viewed as cowards or criminals. Kit Carson, who is honored in American history books as a great scout and pioneer, was a bigoted Mexican-hater and a thief who stole Mexican land in New Mexico for his own purposes. Because he believed that all "greasers" were naturally cowardly and unable to fight an open war, Carson persuaded General Stephen Kearney to invade California with only a fraction of the men he intended to bring. To Kearney's sorrow and Carson's surprise, the Mexicans dealt a decisive (but temporary) defeat to the Americans at the Battle of San Pascual. Kearney was wounded as a result of the battle. Still, Carson's prejudice about Mexicans was shared by other Anglos in the Southwest. The Mexican, it was said, was an expert with the knife because it was the weapon of assassins and cowards. Overlooked was the fact that Mexican *vaqueros,* the West's original cowboys, used the knife as a valuable tool and weapon long before sidearms were in popular use.

Mexican criminals, or Mexicans who acted out of character, were put in their place by lynch mobs or vigilante committees. At times, the strong arm of the law reached out with no less a deadly and completely arbitrary force. Judge Roy Bean and Hanging Judge Parker were famous for their merciless frontier-style "justice," especially toward Mexicans. If Judge Bean, "the Law West of the Pecos," was utterly without mercy, he was not without eloquence as he sentenced a Mexican to death:

> Carlos Robles, you have been tried by twelve true and good men, not men of yore peers, but as high above you as heaven is of hell, and they've said you're guilty of rustlin' cattle.
>
> Time will pass and seasons will come and go; Spring with wavin' green grass and heaps of sweet-smellin' flowers on every hill and in every dale. Then will come sultry Summer, with her shimmerin' heat waves on the baked horizon; and Fall, with her yeller harvest-moon and the hills a-growin' brown and golden under a sinkin' sun; and finally Winter, with its bitin', whinin' wind, and all the land will be mantled with snow.
>
> But you won't be here to see any of 'em, Carlos Robles; not by a dam' sight, because it's the order of this court that you be took to the nearest tree and hanged by the neck till you're dead, dead, you olive-colored son-of-a-billy-goat![7]

And Hanging Judge Parker sentenced another Mexican in similar style:

> And then, José Manual Xavier Gonzales, I command further that such officer or officers retire quietly from your swinging, dangling corpse, that the vultures may descend from the heavens upon your filthy body and pick the putrid flesh therefrom 'til nothing remain but the bare, bleached bones of a cold-blooded, copper-colored, blood-thirsty, chili-eating, guilty, sheep-herding, Mexican son-of-a-bitch.[8]

If in fact the judges actually uttered these sentences, their eloquence was probably wasted on Robles and Gonzales who, at best, understood very little English. What is beyond question is that Mexicans were viewed as foreigners, criminal misfits with no place in American frontier society.

When lynchings ceased in the 1880s, violence still prevailed and Mexican life was cheap, especially along the border. In Texas, famed gunman King Fisher was asked how many notches he had on his gun. He replied: "Thirty-seven—not counting Mexicans."[9] And all Texas Rangers were said to have some Mexican blood—on their boots. *Los Rinches* (Rangers) were formed to keep Mexicans in their place and frequently—in later years—were used as strikebreakers. From the time of the conquest to the turn of the century, it was open season on Mexicans, who remained largely defenseless and vulnerable before *gringo* gunmen and institutions of law and order.

The law thinks of Mexicans as undesirable aliens. This is the constant impression millions of Mexicans have had in dealing with *la migra*. In 1925, the Border Patrol of the United States Immigration and Naturalization Service *(la migra)* was given absolute search and seizure authority over Mexicans. They were authorized to vigorously search out illegal aliens and deport them. Thus, *la migra* was constituted as police, judge, jury, and executioner of wetbacks. Actual experiences with the Border Patrol or fear of being apprehended and deported is possibly the Mexican's most traumatic contact with American law and order—law and order that appears as an unreasonable and unjust form of violence and exclusion.

At times, when the need for wetback labor was great, powerful agriculture lobbies in Washington saw that the Border Patrol's appropriations were kept small to limit patrol manpower and allow the easy flow of wetback laborers across the border. When there ceased to be a need for large numbers of wetbacks, the Border Patrol was strengthened, and not only were strict measures taken to prevent them from crossing the border, but *la migra* sent raiding parties into the *barrios* to terrorize and disrupt the lives of Mexican Americans. In 1953, as a result of the Walter-McCarran Law, 480,000 Mexican wetbacks were deported. On March 3, 1953, the Associated Press issued this report from Fresno, California:

> Three hundred and twenty-five Mexican immigrants—including sixteen women and seven children—were rounded up in a search in which mounted riders and an airplane were used. These three hundred and twenty-five people—hunted down like animals by an airplane and horseback riders—were arrested without warrants, put on a chartered bus and immediately deported to Mexico without any hearings or any semblance of legal procedure.[10]

And in 1954, seven hundred and fifty immigration agents descended on Los Angeles' *barrios,* arresting thousands of Mexicans. Elysian Park, located north of downtown L.A., was converted into a concentration camp where Mexican immigrants arrested in the roundup were kept under close guard. They were soon deported without due process. In that year—1954—over a million Mexicans were deported from the Southwest back to Mexico.[11] (As we have already seen, hundreds of thousands of Mexican people, more than half of whom were American citizens, were deported in the late 1930s and early 1940s as a result of actions by local communities that felt the Mexicans were too great a burden for their welfare rolls.)

Besides wholesale and unjust deportations, Mexicans were exposed to still other forms of injustice and racial prejudice. In the highly publicized 1942 "Sleepy Lagoon Case," several Mexican American boys were convicted of murder by a prejudiced judge and in an atmosphere of race hatred in Los Angeles. The trial provided the city with "a Roman holiday of sensationalism, crime-mongering, and Mexican-baiting."[12] And in 1943 the "Zoot-Suit Riots" were outright acts of racial violence directed against Mexicans for no other reason than the color of their skin and the style of their clothes (many young Mexican Americans of the time wore "zoot suits," loose-fitting, outlandish clothes which were in vogue) and because many white servicemen had nothing better to do than pick a dirty fight with Mexican teenagers.

The violence which lasted several days was condoned and supported by Los Angeles policemen who stood by and did nothing to prevent hundreds of soldiers, sailors, and marines from literally invading East Los Angeles and beating up every zoot-suiter they could find. When the servicemen couldn't find any Mexicans on the streets to "riot" with, they went into movie theaters or stopped streetcars and searched for Mexicans. Those they found were beaten, stripped of their clothing, and, in some cases, their heads were shaved. Later police intervened to arrest the boys who had been beaten. Racial violence against Mexicans during this time became so intense and widespread that the Mexican government formally protested to the United States Department of State. This action had some effect, because for a time the newspapers put a stop to their biased and prejudicial reporting, and the violence subsided. A foreign government, then, had to intervene on behalf of besieged Mexican Americans.[13]

The attitude of the law toward Mexicans has been clearly stated by high-ranking officials in public office. In 1942, the Los Angeles County Sheriff's Department issued an "explanation" of Mexican juvenile delinquency which stated: ". . . his (the Mexican's) desire is to kill, or at least to let blood. . . . This inborn characteristic has come down through the ages."[14] In 1960, the Los Angeles Chief of Police issued this statement:

> The Latin population that came here in great strength were here before us, and presented a great problem because I worked over on the East Side when men had to work in pairs . . . and it's because of some of these people being not too far removed from the wild tribes of the district of the inner mountains of Mexico. I don't think

you can throw the genes out of the question when you discuss behavior patterns of people.[15]

In 1969, Judge Gerald S. Chargin of Santa Clara (California) Juvenile Court proved to be a latter-day "frontier-style" judge when he sentenced a young Chicano for the crime of incest: "We ought to send you back to Mexico. You ought to commit suicide! Hitler was right. The animals in our society ought to be destroyed."[16] And in 1970, the late J. Edgar Hoover was quoted in *Time* magazine as saying, "You never have to bother about a President being shot by a Puerto Rican or Mexicans. They don't shoot very straight. But if they come at you with a knife, beware."[17] Despite many protests from the Chicano community, especially within the last few years, nothing has been done to retract any of these statements or reprimand those who use their high offices to disparage the Mexican character. (In fact, it seems that the evil are rewarded for their deeds. Within a few months after making his infamous statement, Chargin was promoted to a Superior Court judgeship.)

What the law thinks of Mexicans has long been recorded in court pronouncements, police reports, and statements by high-ranking officials. As we have seen, it is based on Anglo-white prejudice supported by myth, stereotype, and hearsay—which, in a sense, does no immediate damage to Chicanos. But in the *barrios,* racial prejudice is recorded not in written or verbal statements but in actual violence and death. And since Salazar's killing, even the most reasonable or moderate Chicanos have come to believe that the police and other officials really mean what they say.

III

THE CHICANO is a man without rights. Overpoliced, prevented from organizing, and without political representation, the Chicano feels trapped and powerless. And no matter where he turns he finds the doors of justice closed against him. Increasingly, millions of other Americans have come to share his alienation—those without money, property, or political influence. But the Chicano, in the eyes of the law, has two more strikes against him: the color of his skin and the language he speaks.

"Mexican Americans are subject to unduly harsh treatment by law enforcement officers," wrote the Rev. Theodore Hesburgh, chairman of the U.S. Civil Rights Commission. "They are often arrested on insufficient grounds, receive physical and verbal abuse and penalties which are disproportionately severe."[18] Prejudicial treatment and harassment of Mexican Americans in the *barrio* has become a way of life. The Denver Legal Aid Society, for instance, reported a case in which a policeman stopped a young Chicano as he was escorting a blonde Anglo girl home from a party. The girl was driving and the officer told her she was speeding. When he noticed the young man next to her, the policeman said, "Mexican, what are you doing with a white woman!" and arrested him. The young man was charged with four traffic violations which were dismissed because the girl testified she was driving. The officer later called the girl's mother to tell her that her daughter was out with a "Mexican."

Cruz Reynoso, formerly the head of California Rural Legal Assistance (CRLA) and now a professor at the University of New Mexico Law School, told me that similar verbal and even physical abuse occur wherever there are *barrios* and cited an example of grim *barrio* humor: "I'd rather meet a robber than a cop in a dark alley. The robber will beat you up, rob you, and leave you half-dead. But the cop will beat you up, rob you, and throw you in jail."

One reason for the disproportionate abuse and harassment is that police deployment is based on the presumption that *barrios* are full of criminals. In other words, police presume that if you are poor and brown, living in the *barrio,* you are likely to be a criminal in need of intense and tough policing. According to the findings of police–community relations expert Armando Morales, the double standard is at work in the *barrio*. Morales, an assistant professor in the Department of Psychiatry at the University of California, Los Angeles, made a comparison of police deployment practices for East Los Angeles and West Valley, a white neighborhood with a comparable population. The ratio of major crimes per population was about the same (4.9 percent). Yet more police are assigned to East Los Angeles (13.5 officers per square mile) than to the predominantly Anglo-white area (3.5 officers per square mile). If self-fulfilling predictions continue to be realized it is because overpolicing leads to more arrests.[19] According to unofficial estimates, 52 percent of the 61,000 juveniles arrested in Los Angeles County in 1969 were Chicanos, most of whom came from East Los Angeles.

Chicanos have lodged hundreds of complaints against police for alleged misconduct but to little or no avail. Many of these complaints are processed through the ACLU Police Malpractice Complaint Center in East Los Angeles. Art Garcia, director for the Center, told me, "The situation in our *barrio* couldn't get any worse. Police come in and kick us around and when someone complains, he can't get any satisfaction." Complaints against police can only be lodged with the police themselves, who, in turn, are increasingly defensive about their activities in the *barrio*. Garcia has investigated many of the complaint cases and finds that the most frequent complaint is extreme physical abuse (two or more blows by police on an unresisting civilian). An explosive situation exists in the *barrio* that is instantly triggered by contact between Chicanos and white policemen or sheriff's deputies. Chicanos know from long experience that they will often be arbitrarily arrested for "investigation" purposes, subjected to humiliating "stop and frisk" searches, or harassed in other ways. They resent such treatment and often resist it. Thus many of the young Chicanos arrested in the *barrio* are invariably charged with one or more of the following crimes: (1) disturbing the peace, (2) resisting an officer, and (3) assault of an officer. Significantly, two of these three crimes could only happen *after* police arrived on the scene.[20]

During 1970–1971, East L.A. was the most riot-torn area in the nation. Clashes between Chicanos and police seemed to be the immediate cause for the disturbances. (As we have already seen, the underlying causes for the violence directed at stores and businesses were socioeconomic in nature.) In the disturbances during this period, as in the urban riots during the mid 1960s, a distinct pattern emerged. Armando Morales, in his Chicano-police riot analysis, reported that there were three phases: (1) police are stoned, crowds collect, and tension builds; (2) store windows are broken and looting begins; (3) further violence escalates—arson, firebombing. Police then respond in full force and Chicanos confront them in the streets. Morales notes in his analysis of the August 29, 1970, riot,* that the Chicano-police confrontation occurred *before* the riot on Whittier Boulevard. This strongly suggests that the overreaction of police triggered the riot![21] Police have become symbols of all that the Chicano feels is oppressing him. In the *barrio* they have come to be viewed as an occupational force of enemies.

Besides feelings of alienation and powerlessness which they share with other oppressed minorities, Chicanos have an added problem: at times they cannot communicate with the police or authorities. Actually, it is a police problem, for they are often unprepared and insensitive to the needs of Spanish-speaking citizens. The U.S. Civil Rights Commission in 1968 told of a Mexican American who was held for two months in an Arizona jail for allegedly molesting his small daughter. Apparently the man had been mistakenly arrested,

*Morales's *Ando Sangrando (I Am Bleeding): A Study of Mexican American–Police Conflict* (1972) is the best available treatment of Chicano-police conflict and its underlying causes. Unfortunately, Morales's original manuscript was repeatedly rejected by white publishers who claimed that it was "too powerful" and "indigestible for the Anglo reader." *Ando Sangrando* was rejected by 17 major publishers until Morales finally published it at his own expense. Consciously or not, the white press often reflects, as Morales has said, "the biases of white America in failing to inform and educate the whole of society."

but the charges were never explained to him in his own language. Only two months later, when a Spanish-speaking parole officer spoke with the man were the actual facts of the case made known. The local magistrate immediately dismissed the case.[22] While conditions vary from state to state, the United States Civil Rights Commission found that "equal protection of the law is being withheld from Mexican Americans on a widespread basis because of the inability to communicate between Spanish-speaking citizens and English-speaking officials."[23]

The law has done everything imaginable to prevent Chicanos from organizing themselves. The labor movement among Mexican Americans in the early part of this century is a good example of this interference. More recently, as we have already seen, the leaders of the 1968 East L.A. "Blow Outs" were indicted on conspiracy charges by the district attorney for no other apparent motive than the harassment of Chicano leaders and to place a chilling effect on future protests by Chicanos against school conditions.

Reies Tijerina's *Alianza Federal de Mercedes* and César Chavez's UFWOC have also been the objects of repeated attempts by police and government to stop them from being effective. Police in New Mexico described the *Alianza* as a "Communist-front" organization, and the district attorney of Rio Arriba County continually harassed *Alianza* leaders and members. Meetings were disrupted and those who attended were arrested and denied due process. A flagrant instance of this occurred in Canjilon, New Mexico, on June 5, 1967. All those present at an *Alianza* meeting—men, women, and children—were arrested by a troop of eighty state policemen and held for more than twenty-four hours without adequate shelter or drinking water while they were kept under guard by four hundred and fifty national guardsmen. Their crime was in being associated with an organization demanding the return of stolen lands to their rightful owners. Tijerina was later tried for the crime of "burning a forest-service sign" and has just been released after serving a two-year sentence.

Tijerina's conviction and jail sentence are clearly a case of selective enforcement of the laws (most *gringos* would have received a $25 fine and a suspended sentence for doing the same thing). The New Mexico courts either refused to hear or rejected his appeals; he served the full two years as a political prisoner.

During the 1966–1967 period in Starr County, Texas, *los rinches* (better known as the Texas Rangers) were called in as strikebreakers when César Chavez's UFWOC tried to organize the farmworkers in the area. The Rangers have a reputation for being brutal in their treatment of Mexicans, and their very presence is often enough to discourage many Chicanos from participating in legitimate strike activities. One farmworker testified before the Civil Rights Commission: "When the Rangers are coming, then the people are afraid. They are afraid of being hit, or being pushed around. . . . The minute that you hear the Rangers are coming, then they don't want to strike. This is the feeling of the people in the Valley. They are afraid."[24]

Chicanos who protest before the local or federal bar of justice are not likely to be heard. This is especially true in the state of Texas. In March of 1970, for example, the U.S. Civil Rights Commission disclosed that the Justice Department had closed its investigative files in a case involving a Mexican American who was shot and killed by a San Antonio policeman. The reason given by Justice officials was that "prosecution of a white police officer for shooting a Mexican would have little chance of success in the southern district of Texas."[25] In the Fall of 1970, the Los Angeles district attorney used the same reasoning when he refused to indict the man who killed Ruben Salazar: "the unlikelihood of a unanimous jury."[26] Such failures to prosecute in emotionally charged cases only deepens and aggravates the Chicano's mistrust and disrespect for the law. And this disrespect is further heightened when the double standard of selective prosecution becomes apparent. While the "unlikelihood of a unanimous jury" is used as an excuse to absolve police officers of being tried for crimes, Chicanos who have been charged (especially with alleged crimes against police) have been tried two and three times after the first trials ended in hung juries.[27]

When cases involving Chicanos finally get to court, it is often likely that they will not receive a fair, impartial hearing. Grand and petit juries in the Southwest are so unrepresentative of Chicanos that it is similar to the jury exclusion of blacks in the South.[28] Chicano lawyer Oscar Zeta Acosta in 1970 challenged this systematic exclusion as practiced in the selection of jurors for the Los Angeles County Grand Jury. Acosta contended that in the previous ten years a mere token three Chicanos from a total of two hundred and ten grand jurors served on the County Grand Jury—that is 1.9 percent from an overall 13 percent of the Chicanos in Los Angeles County. In March 1971, the Los Angeles Superior Court ruled against his challenge. Chicanos were not deliberately or systematically excluded, ruled the court, "because in each of the ten years at least one Mexican American was nominated for jury duty." But the fact remained that Chicanos were (and continue to be) excluded while an "elitist, stacked body summoned to protect the interest of the most wealthy, the most intelligent, the most successful [of white society]" are called to serve.[29] "This shows," said Acosta after the court ruled against him, "that Chicanos can't get justice in the courtroom."[30]

Another Chicano lawyer fighting for justice is Mario Obledo of the Mexican American Legal and Education Defense Fund (MALDEF). "I want to stay within the system," Obledo told me, "but how can you expect justice from judges who don't know our people or understand our problems?" With a small staff of lawyers, MALDEF covers the Southwest from offices in San Antonio, Los Angeles, and San Francisco. It has more than three hundred cases pending in court, many of them dealing with law reform, class actions, and police malpractice cases. "We have to fight for every inch of ground," says Obledo. "In many instances you know the judge before you is a racist. You know he's not listening. Why do they let us spend our time and money on appeals!"

The fight is a lonely one for lawyers like Acosta and Obledo. They are among a handful of Chicano lawyers (about six hundred) serving a Chicano population in excess of ten million. According to the Civil Rights Commission only 1.5 percent of all attorneys in California and Texas are Mexican Americans. In Arizona and Colorado the figure is less than one percent. Chicano judges, district attorneys, and other high officials are rare indeed. But where the underrepresentation hurts the most is in the field of law enforcement. The Chicano's image of the law is that of a white policeman or deputy sheriff. He never sees Chicanos in police uniform. This underrepresentation prevails among the two hundred and forty-three police departments in the Southwest.

Many Chicanos are kept out of police work because of the language barrier—the verbal and written tests their lack of education or third-rate *barrio* education has prepared them to fail. Yet it is precisely what bars them—their Mexican background, language, et cetera—that could be of real use in the *barrio*. On the other hand, many Chicanos who could qualify for police work stay away from it because of the *vendido* (sell-out) image it would give them.

Can anything be done to meet the present crisis in police-community relations, or must we face the violent consequences of a steadily worsening situation?

What should be done on the local, state, and federal levels is well known to all, for it has been the subject of countless studies, commission reports, and research projects. In the very recent past, both the U.S. Civil Rights Commission of 1970 and Professor Armando Morales, in his study of Mexican American–police conflict, *Ando Sangrando* (1972), reached the same conclusions as to what must be done to defuse an already smoldering situation between police and Chicanos in the *barrio*.

There must be stronger federal enforcement against civil rights violations. If the district attorney fails to prosecute, the

U.S. Justice Department should act, even if they must by-pass the federal grand jury system. And the possibility of recrimination against federal officials who do act—as in the case of U.S. Attorney Robert L. Meyer—must be guarded against as much as possible. At this point any conviction of civil rights violations would be a historic first, because no Chicano has ever received federal protection against police brutality that resulted in conviction since the law (18 U.S.C. 242) was enacted in 1872.[31] The Federal Jury Selection and Service Act of 1968, which excludes discrimination of minorities, should immediately replace the current outmoded, prejudicial methods of jury selection. The entire bail system must be revamped, and injustices in arraignment, pre-trial, trial, and sentencing procedures must be drastically reformed. And so long as police investigate themselves, Chicanos and other oppressed groups will look upon the whole procedure as a travesty of justice.

Morales also recommends that regular meetings should be conducted between police officials and *barrio* communities to determine the particular community's needs. He asserts that discriminatory police practices should be identified and corrected by keeping careful statistics of arrests by region and ethnic group. And more and more Chicanos should be recruited for law enforcement and justice work. Too often a young Chicano is arrested by a white officer, held in custody because he cannot pay the cash bail, brought before a white judge in a courtroom where often there is no adequate translation service provided; an unrepresentative Anglo-white jury convicts him, and he is sent to a jail or prison that is overcrowded with other Chicanos and run by white guards and officials. Justice must surely appear as a white-dominated system of repression to the very people it purports to serve and protect.

Long-range goals must be implemented, says Morales, which would make political representation a reality. For years the *barrios* have been so gerrymandered that only the needs of the Democratic Party have been served. That was the main reason for Ricardo Romo's candidacy in 1970, as we saw before. More than a million Mexicans live in the city of Los Angeles, and not one Chicano sits on the city council. Representation in Sacramento (California's seat of government) and Washington, D.C., are virtually nonexistent. Until Chicanos have an active voice in creating their own political destiny, every other action to ease tensions will amount to nothing more than Band Aids for a patient suffering from internal disease.

To most Americans, the institutions of law and justice are essential in a society which cherishes and protects the rights of its citizens. But to Chicanos, blacks, and other minority groups, the law often appears as "irrelevant except as a clumsy technique for maintaining order."[32] The law has failed to keep faith with the Chicano community by denying them equality of treatment and protection. Ultimately, however, it is not the law but white society that must bear the responsibility.

The American people will not be judged by the ideals they honored in such documents as the Constitution or Bill of Rights; nor will their true character as a people be manifested by brilliant scientific achievements in the laboratory or in outer space. Who the American people are is unerringly told in how they have treated Chicanos, blacks, and other poor people in this country.

Do Americans have the wisdom and strength to demand change now? Do they have the compassion and sense of justice to look at what is happening all around them? Do they have the courage and humility to look truly within themselves? Can't they see that we are all perishing?

Since Salazar, many Chicanos say no.

NOTES

1. *Los Angeles Free Press,* August 13, 1971.

2. *Los Angeles Times,* October 16, 1970; also see D. F. Gomez, "The Killing of Ruben Salazar," *The Christian Century* (January 13, 1971), pp. 49 ff.

3. See *Los Angeles Times* coverage, October 12–16, 1970.

4. *Los Angeles Times* (Pt. II, p. 6), October 7, 1970.

5. *Los Angeles Times,* August 10, 1971.

6. Leonard Pitt, *The Decline of the Californios* (Berkeley and Los Angeles: University of California Press, 1966), p. 162.

7. B. A. Botkin, editor, *A Treasury of American Folklore* (New York: Crown Publishers, 1944), p. 136; quoted in Francisco Armando Rios, "The Mexican in Fact, Fiction and Folklore," *Voices: Readings from El Grito* (Berkeley: Quinto Sol Publications, Inc., 1971), pp. 59–73.

8. B. A. Botkin, *op. cit.,* p. 148, as cited by Rios, *op. cit.*

9. Carey McWilliams, *North from Mexico* (New York: Greenwood Press, Publishers, 1968), p. 98, as quoted by Rios, *op. cit.*

10. Quoted in Louise Pettibone Smith's *Torch of Liberty* (New York: Dwight-King Publishers, Inc., 1959), p. 420.

11. *Ibid.*

12. Carey McWilliams, *op. cit.,* p. 230 ff.

13. Armando Morales, *Ando Sangrando (I Am Bleeding): A Study of Mexican American–Police Conflict* (La Puente, California: Perspectiva Publications, 1972), p. 17.

14. McWilliams, *op. cit.,* p. 234, quoted in Leo Grebler, Joan W. Moore, Ralph C. Guzman, *The Mexican American People: The Nation's Second Largest Minority* (New York: The Free Press, 1970), p. 529.

15. Grebler, Moore, and Guzman, *op. cit.,* p. 530.

16. "Judge Gerald S. Chargin Speaks," *El Grito* (Vol. II, No. 1, Fall 1969), pp. 4 ff.

17. *Time* Magazine (December 14, 1970), cited by Morales, *op. cit.,* p. 44.

18. United States Civil Rights Commission, *Mexican Americans and the Administration of Justice in the Southwest* (Washington, D.C., March 1970), p. iii.

19. Morales, *op. cit.,* pp. 54, 49 ff.

20. *Ibid.*, p. 29; also see D. F. Gomez, "Chicanos: Strangers in Their Own Land," *America* (Vol. 124, No. 25), June 26, 1971, p. 651.

21. Armando Morales, "Chicano-Police Riots," in *Chicanos: Social and Psychological Perspectives,* edited by Nathaniel N. Wagner and Marsha J. Haug (St. Louis: The C. V. Mosby Co., 1971), pp. 184–202.

22. Ruben Salazar, *Stranger in One's Own Land* (Washington, D.C., May 1970), p. 38.

23. *Mexican Americans and the Administration of Justice,* p. iii.

24. Salazar, *op. cit.*, pp. 41–42.

25. *Mexican Americans and the Administration of Justice,* pp. 32–33.

26. Morales, *Ando Sangrando,* p. 73.

27. *Ibid.*

28. *Mexican Americans and the Administration of Justice,* p. 40.

29. Oscar Zeta Acosta, "The East L.A. 13 vs. the L.A. Superior Court," *El Grito* (Winter 1970), p. 16.

30. *Los Angeles Times* (Part I, p. 3), April 1, 1971.

31. Morales, *Ando Sangrando,* p. 20.

32. Ramsey Clark, *Crime in America* (New York: Pocket Books, 1970), p. 229.

CHAPTER SEVEN

El Movimiento Chicano

CHICANOS HAVE LEARNED the lessons of history. We have been in this country—our country—long enough to have identified the enemy. The enemy is variously labeled *"gabacho,"* "Anglo society," "the Man," et cetera. The name is not important. The reality behind the labels is a system which creates desperately impoverished and underprivileged people on a regular basis. Invariably these poor people are Chicanos, blacks, and other visible minorities.

The Chicano movement is the collective understanding and concerted effort by Chicanos to eradicate the causes of our widespread poverty, discrimination, and economic oppression. By whatever means necessary! The analysts of nationalistic movements like to chart the progression of a militant people through stages of collective consciousness.* To some extent, this pattern is valid for Chicanos.

First, there is the primitive consciousness that nothing can be done about our plight. People come to think that poverty is a way of life, an undeniable fact that we must adjust ourselves to. A subtle variation of this attitude, one expressed by middle-class Mexican Americans, is that while poverty is indeed always with us, any Chicano can "make it" in Anglo society if he works hard enough and pulls himself up by his own bootstraps.

*See, for example, Paulo Freire's excellent work, *Pedagogy of the Oppressed* (New York: Herder and Herder, 1972).

Secondly, there is the naive consciousness that although we've somehow been victimized, the blame as well as the solution rests with others. And so the people look to the government, the churches, poverty programs, et cetera, as their salvation. In the early stages of the movement, many Chicanos hid themselves behind posters of Emiliano Zapata and Pancho Villa, as if those dead warriors could now win victories for them in twentieth century Anglo society. We had not yet learned to trust ourselves and one another.

The final stage is when the people stop looking to others for their liberation and come to the critical awareness not only of who has been victimizing them, but also of the fact that the power for liberation resides with the people. No one else. Leaders, the new Zapatas and Villas, will emerge when the people start fighting for their own cause.

Chicanos have been reaching this critical consciousness in ever-increasing numbers. This chapter illustrates how this Movement consciousness has provoked Chicano Catholics to overcome their early childhood fears and so-called religious training to challenge the most powerful church in this country and the world; how Chicano lawyers have repudiated Anglo values they learned in law school and have started to fight as part of the people; and how an obscure Chicano from East L.A. sacrificed his freedom and risked his life for the cause of Chicano liberation.

I

How many churches, let alone million-dollar churches, did Christ build? We looked further and found that, although as a matter of faith all of us are members of the Catholic Church, nonetheless no Chicanos are able to participate in decisions within the Church, which are not of purely religious nature. Would you have voted for a million-dollar church? As Mexican-Americans, as Católicos, as Chicanos, it is our fault if the Catholic Church in the Southwest is no longer a Church of blood, a Church of struggle, a Church of sacrifice. It is our fault because we have not raised our voices as Catholics and as poor people for the love of Christ. We can't love our people without demanding better housing, education, health, and so many other needs we share in common.

—*Open letter from CPLR to the people of the barrios*

The conflict between the Catholic Church and the Chicano was dramatically, almost surrealistically, acted out in violent confrontation on Christmas Eve 1969, in St. Basil's Church, Los Angeles.

The open conflict began to develop in the Fall of that year when Chicano activists, many of them college and university students and members of *Mecha,* raised the issue of the Church's flagrant neglect of its oldest, most faithful, and largest racial minority in the Southwest. "Any fool could see," said one of the *Mechistas,* "that the Catholic Church has done nothing for our people."

The activists, who called themselves *Católicos por la Raza* (CPLR), i.e., Catholics for the People, had little trouble proving their point. The Church, ever since the Southwest was annexed, has approached Mexican American people with the same colonialist, missionary attitude which motivated the Franciscan friars in their evangelization of the Indians during the mission era.

An instance of this approach is that there have never been many native Chicano vocations. In other words, Mexican Americans would have to be *gringo*ized (and very few of them were) to the point that the Church would seem attractive as a framework for a lifetime of ministry and service. Moreover, the Southwest Church has been dominated by French, German, and mainly Irish priests in top leadership positions, despite the fact that there have always been able Mexican or Mexican American priests available. Needless to say, the Irish, non–Spanish-speaking priests and bishops have traditionally been unable to fully identify with the needs, aspirations, and best interests of Chicanos.

And Chicanos, along with Indians, were treated like

irresponsible children. The Church patronized them instead of defending them. The Church preached passivity and acceptance instead of resistance against evil. And they practiced what they preached: during the repatriations in the 1930s, the Church made no protest at the illegal and unconstitutional deportations of Mexican Americans. During the 1940s, the Church stood by silently while Chicano youth were made the object of a concerted campaign of racist propaganda and overt violence.

Besides recalling history, CPLR did extensive research into the Church's assets and came up with some startling statistics that most Catholic lay people and even priests would not be aware of. Through research into title records, they discovered that the Church owned property totaling more than a billion dollars in Los Angeles County alone.

This figure included churches, parochial schools, and convents, but four out of six of the properties listed were non-church related. These were businesses and residences which included a variety of holdings from slum property in the Pico-Union area to exclusive hi-rise apartments in Beverly Hills and West Los Angeles. "The Church is filthy wealthy," said one of the *Católicos,* "and it can say what it wants about the property not being negotiable or in liquid assets, yet the fact is that they have the land and that means power."

In 1969, the spiritual leader of Los Angeles's two million Catholics and the guardian of the billion dollars in real property was 83-year-old James Francis Cardinal McIntyre. *Católicos por la Raza* arranged an initial meeting with him in early September and another meeting was subsequently held in November. (At the second meeting, the *Católicos* had to push their way past the Cardinal's priest-secretaries because he had refused to see them at first.) "Both times we met," said Joe Razo, one of the CPLR spokesmen, "they said they sympathized with the Chicano's problems but that there was no money for the programs we proposed. Yet we knew they had given the blacks money. We told the Cardinal, 'If you're able to give the blacks money and we are a larger population, 65 percent of the Catholic population in the Southwest, then why don't you service the people through community action-oriented programs?'"

McIntyre told the group on both occasions that there was no money and even if there were, the Church could not get involved in such programs because the Church is apolitical. The only kind of programs being funded, he said, were like the mission downtown for derelicts and alcoholics. He also said the Church had already done a great deal for Chicanos by building parochial schools in the *barrios*. Which in fact was true. CPLR challenged this, however, because they said that Catholic schools, hospitals, et cetera were as racist and inadequate as similar public institutions. Which also was true.

"When the Cardinal told us, 'We give Easter baskets and Christmas baskets,'" said Joe Razo, "we challenged him again. The Church is a hope-maker. They give people hope by giving them a Christmas basket, hope that things will change next year. And sure as hell, next year the Church is bringing the same Christmas basket again. And they're giving hope but no social change just like the welfare, you give people a check and they hope things will change by next check but it doesn't. And it's just sucking them up on their hopes and aspirations and makes no political change."

Despite the Cardinal's statement to the contrary, the Church has never hesitated to enter the political arena, using whatever influence it has, whether to influence antiabortion legislation or state aid to parochial school education. What most angered the *Católicos* was that while Cardinal McIntyre was disavowing any involvement with political matters, he had recently invited Governor Ronald Reagan and President-elect Richard M. Nixon (both accepted) to a $100-a-plate fund-raising dinner for the Archdiocese.

The central issue that emerged from the two encounters with the Cardinal and other chancery officials was whether or not the Catholic Church in Los Angeles, with its tremendous wealth and power, would do anything for the political and social involvement of the Chicano people. The Cardinal from that point on refused to see the activists and labeled them "militants" and "rabble." At this point also the CPLR activists took to the streets with protests and demonstrations. They picketed the chancery office, and soon St. Basil's Church, a recently built, ultramodern church, the size of a basilica or cathedral, became the focal point of dissent. St. Basil's had cost four million dollars to build and was intended to be the Cardinal's showpiece for special occasions.

On the Sunday prior to Christmas Eve, CPLR staged a protest in front of the large church. About two hundred demonstrators stood outside with placards denouncing the Church's wealth and affluence, singing songs in Spanish *("Estas Son Las Mañanitas"),* and passing out leaflets to passers-by. At the end of the protest, the group's leaders told the Cardinal's representatives inside the rectory that unless their demands for more Chicano programs were met, they would be back again—and not to sing *"Estas Son Las Mañanitas*"! There was no apparent response from the Cardinal.

On Christmas Eve, at about 11:00 P.M., CPLR met in front of the chancery office on Ninth Street. About four to five hundred people showed up. Candles were distributed to all present, and a candlelight procession began wending its way toward St. Basil's, a few blocks to the north. The participants were mostly young Chicano students, but a great many family people—mothers, fathers, grandmothers, even infants—were also in attendance. Among the Chicano students, there were several *veteranos*, seasoned campaigners in the Chicano movement. For instance, at the head of the procession was a tall, heavy-set Chicano dressed almost completely in black. On his shirt, he wore several movement buttons ("Chicano Power," "Boycott Grapes," "Free Sal Castro," et cetera) in much the same way a soldier proudly displays campaign ribbons. Chosen as the standard bearer, he carried a large banner of *La Virgen Mestiza, La Madre de la Revolución.**

When the procession reached the church, they staged their own Mass in Spanish, on the church steps. Three priests (all Anglos) who sympathized with the Chicano group, celebrated the eucharist. As this service of breaking bread was being conducted, people began arriving to attend Midnight Mass inside the church. CPLR people passed out leaflets and, by being present in front of the church in such a large group, made clear their point that Chicanos were critical of the rich white man's church.

By the time the *Católicos'* Mass outside had finished, the Mass inside was about to begin. Richard Cruz, CPLR Cochairman, gave a short talk from the steps of the church, reminding the people of the Church's hypocrisy in building a four million dollar church while saying they were on the side of the poor. He also pointed out the symbolism of the *Católicos* being on the street while the white parishioners, most of them upper-middle-class types, were inside the sumptuous church. "The church is ours because we're Catholics, too, and anyone who wants to go to Mass can go to Mass," he said. "But we're through out here. So anyone who wants to go home, go home." Everyone stayed.

Then a nucleus of about fifty went up the concrete steps to enter the front doors of the church but found the heavy glass outer doors locked. "The thing was locked up real tight, like a coffin," said one participant. "And that's where it all started." The four to five hundred people outside, all of whom were Catholics, became very angry and frustrated because the doors had been locked against them. It was an insult to them, said one, because it was like calling them "rabble" or

*Our Lady of Guadalupe, according to Mexican Catholic tradition, appeared in a vision to Juan Diego, an *Indio,* in 1521. She appeared as a *mestiza,* a racial mixture of Spanish and Indian. Thus, as the *Mestiza* mother of God, she is the chief symbol and source of Mexican religiosity as well as a unifying symbol to Mexican people during times of adversity or revolution. Under her patronage and banner, peasants fought against Spaniards in 1810; and the armies of Zapata revered her as their patroness during the revolution of 1910.

"troublemakers" who couldn't be trusted inside the church. The people began to shout for someone to open the doors and let them enter.

At this point, a white nun, a sister of the Immaculate Heart Order, who was inside worshiping at the back of the church, heard the noise and went back to see what was going on. She asked the ushers, who seemed to be standing guard at the large doors, "Why don't you let the poor people in?" And the Chicanos on the other side of the doors took up the cry, "Let the poor people in!" Soon all the demonstrators were chanting, "Let the poor people in!" And the sound of the chanting could be heard inside the church and was even picked up on the sound system of the television crews who were televising the Mass.

During the chanting, Chicanos went around to the side of the church looking for an entrance and found a way in. They went to the back of the church and opened the doors from inside. But when one of the Chicanos opened the doors, he was jumped from behind by one of the ushers. The ushers, it turned out, were undercover sheriff's deputies who later claimed they were "off duty." While they may have been officially off duty, each of them was fully armed with service revolver, night stick, handcuffs, and can of mace. As a burly deputy jumped the Chicano from behind, other deputies joined in to prevent the demonstrators from entering, but it was too late. The people had already started to stream in.

All of the ushers went to the back of the church with their night sticks drawn and cans of mace ready to use. They tried to force the people out of the church and only succeeded in starting a number of fights with the angry Chicanos who were determined not to be thrown out of their church. By this time the Gospel of the Nativity was being intoned by one of the priests in the sanctuary. Because of the chanting and noise from the fighting and scuffling in the back, the priest summoned two other priests to join in unison with him reciting the Gospel. In this way, they tried to drown out the sounds of the people being beaten by the deputies.

At this time, a prearranged signal had been given for the Los Angeles Police Department's crack riot squad to come to the aid of the deputies. Apparently the Cardinal had made special plans for stopping trouble before it could develop, because the riot squad troopers had been secretly hidden from view in the Cardinal's personal quarters at the rear of the church. Two full units took only moments to arrive on the scene. And they came dressed for action—helmets, face shields, riot sticks. They streamed into the vestibule, striking first with their riot sticks and asking questions later.

While this confrontation escalated with the arrival of the riot squad, Cardinal McIntyre, dressed in red velvet robes and seated on the high episcopal throne inside the sanctuary, did not once look toward the source of the disturbance but kept his eyes on the Mass as it continued without interruption.

The vestibule or antechamber was the battlefield that evening and morning. In St. Basil's, the vestibule is exceptionally large and can accommodate three to four hundred standing people. By the time the riot squad had arrived their work was cut out for them, because most of the demonstrators had gotten into the vestibule. The officers beat the people back into the street and allowed no one to get into the main part of the church. (The television cameras never caught a glimpse of what was happening, although the TV audience could plainly hear the battle sounds from the vestibule for a full fifteen minutes.) The demonstrators were beaten, kicked, clubbed, and maced by police in an effort to get them out into the street again.

The noises grew so loud that Monsignor Benjamin Hawks, who was acting as Master of Ceremonies, again attempted to drown out the anguished screams of the people by having the congregation sing (ironically) "O Come, All Ye Faithful"!

"They pushed us out onto the sidewalk," said Joe Razo. "I saw one person being beaten by three cops, and I went over there and before you know it, I got hit. Whacked me on the head and knocked me down. The first thing I did was bundle up and I tried to crawl under a car. And I heard one of the cops say, 'Give that bastard another head-shot.' And I was defenseless, I wasn't struggling. I was trying to protect my head. And before you know it, the lights went out. That head-shot took sixteen stitches." Another participant said, "I saw a pregnant woman down and being kicked. But I couldn't get over to help her."

Meanwhile, back in the church, Cardinal McIntyre was still absorbed in the Mass as worshipers approached the altar to receive holy communion.

Still more police reinforcements were called in. About twenty-one arrests were made and the remaining two to three hundred demonstrators were pushed down Wilshire Boulevard by club-swinging police until the crowd was dispersed. In the church, as the Mass ended, Cardinal McIntyre addressed the congregation for the first time: "We are ashamed of the participants and we recognize that their conduct was symbolic of the conduct of the rabble as they stood at the foot of the cross, shouting, 'Crucify him!'" Then he told the people, "Forgive them for they know not what they do."

"So that night and later," said Richard Cruz, "the whole posture and approach of the parishioners, Cardinal, and police was that we were 'rabble.' It was a once-in-a-lifetime type thing. I have been in lots of riots, you see riots and you can see them for what they are—individuals and passion and turmoil. But you don't always see the issue so clearly. Here you see Jesus being used like crazy, being used not by some flunky priest who's afraid of anybody, but by the Cardinal. It was a mind-blower, like seeing some sort of fantastic painting, or something like that, where you could see theory, political action, philosophy, and religion all at once."

While the Cardinal had generously made reference to Jesus's words of forgiveness, there was no forgiveness for those arrested or later charged. At first they were booked on conspiracy charges, but when the district attorney could not gather enough evidence for that, the charges became the misdemeanor of disrupting a religious service. In subsequent trials, only seven persons were actually found guilty and sentenced to ninety days in the county jail.

"McIntyre should have stood trial, not us," says Richard Cruz. "He incited to riot that night! If there's anyone who should have gone to jail it was the Cardinal. If the church doors had been open, only a few angry Chicanos might have gone in and said something or been otherwise so pissed off at the pomp and circumstance that they would have done something. So here you go and lock the doors and the police and riot squad are waiting in ambush for us; and we come in with our mothers and sisters and babies! And who laid the ambush? Cardinal McIntyre!"

In the aftermath of the Christmas Eve incident, *Católicos por la Raza* brought the issues of conflict into clearer focus by publishing and distributing in the *barrios* 200,000 copies of a four-page tabloid which factually itemized the Church's immense holdings in Los Angeles County and asked the readers to draw their own conclusions. The tabloid was printed in both Spanish and English. Mexican Americans, many of them unsympathetic to the irreverent troublemakers (as the press depicted them) were nevertheless drawn into the debate because the facts and figures spoke for themselves. Many went to their local parish priests and asked, "Father, is it true about the property?" The Church responded by using the Archdiocesan paper, *The Tidings,* to rebut the charges of hypocrisy. And the debate continued in that vein for two or three months.

Many observers still question whether *Católicos por la Raza* accomplished anything by their conflict with the institutional Church. Many will say it was good for emotional uplift but produced nothing substantial. Perhaps one reason people have been reluctant to give CPLR credit for anything is that the white press dismissed them as "rabble" and "agitators." Another reason is that the Church never admitted any wrongdoing or accepted any fault for the events which developed on Christmas Eve. The implication was that the CPLR was totally responsible for the bodily injuries, destruction of Church property, and arrests.

Directly or indirectly, however, *Católicos por la Raza* were responsible for the following:

The Fund for Human Development. This fund was started a few months after the incident at St. Basil's as a direct response to the CPLR charge that the Church had done nothing for the Chicanos in their struggle for self-determination. It is a nationwide collection taken up on a yearly basis in Catholic parishes in the United States. The money is distributed from a national office in Washington, D.C., to grassroots organizations with almost no strings attached. Most of the money has gone to Chicano groups like Chicano Health Organization, *Abogados de Aztlan,* and so on.

Apparently the Church was afraid that the discontent would grow among Chicano Catholics. Indeed several churches—Catholic and Protestant—had been liberated by Chicano militants in the months following the Christmas Eve confrontation in Los Angeles. The Church wanted to take no chances of a trend starting in which they would continually be put in an embarrassing position. The fund was conscience money being offered to people who had accused the bishops and priests of hypocrisy; it was also a way to neutralize criticism and stem the growing tide of militant rebellion within the fold.

Resolution of the Grape Boycott. In 1969, the U.S. Conference of Catholic Bishops had entered the grape boycott dispute between César Chavez's UFWOC and the growers in Delano as a liaison. But the Church had not been pursuing a negotiated settlement with the influence and power at its disposal. According to CPLR spokesman Richard Martinez: "Some of us talked to César Chavez in Delano several months later and he said, 'If it wasn't for you people, although I may not agree with your tactics, the Church wouldn't have pushed so adamantly for a resolution.'" Six months after the St. Basil's affair, the grape boycott and strike were settled and the Church was rightly given much credit for helping to engineer negotiations.

Appointment of Chicano or Spanish-surnamed Bishops. In 1969, there was not a single Chicano bishop in the United States, nor had there ever been a Chicano member of the U.S. Catholic hierarchy. In the wake of the CPLR demand for representation, Bishop Patrick Flores was installed as auxiliary bishop of San Antonio, Texas. Also, Bishop Juan Arzube, an Ecuadorian by birth, was installed as auxiliary bishop of Los Angeles.

Cardinal McIntyre was forced to retire as head of the Los Angeles Archdiocese. Most of the speculation and educated guesses point to Cardinal McIntyre's being retired because of the bad publicity the Church received on Christmas Eve as well as his advanced age. Complaints were said to have been lodged in Rome, and the papal nuncio was also said to have suggested retirement to the Cardinal. "The reason they got rid of Cardinal McIntyre in my opinion," said Richard Cruz, "was because he was such a lousy tactician. As I said, he incited to riot that night and that doesn't look good for the Cardinal or the Church." Whatever the specific reason, McIntyre was retired, and Archbishop Timothy Manning was appointed to assume control of the Archdiocese. The atmosphere has greatly changed because Manning relates more easily to Chicanos.

Chicanos became more critically aware of their Church and of themselves. The major impact of the demonstrations and demands was the profound and far-reaching effect within the *barrios* and within Chicano families. The week of the Christmas Eve affair, almost every Chicano family had an argument about the nature of the Catholic Church and its role within the Chicano community. Even though it was the young on one side and the older parents and relatives on the other, families stayed together, discussed together, and as a result were stronger families for it.

Many Chicanos who grew up in fear and trembling at the Church and Church officials, were no longer afraid. They had stood their ground, challenged the Church, and made their demands known. And no lightning came down. Many liberal priests and nuns also had to take a stand for or against the Church and the *Católicos por la Raza*. "There's no end to the type of things that happen when men look critically at their church," one activist told me.

What CPLR accomplished, while very great in light of their small numbers, was only a beginning. Indeed most of the monies and programs and appointments have amounted to little more than token concessions. As one veteran activist put it: "The hierarchy still has not made a major decision to support the national liberation struggle of the Chicano people as a nationally oppressed minority." Chicanos remain the most neglected and forgotten people within the Church.

Chicano priests, moreover, are still passed over or ignored when bishops are chosen to head dioceses with large Mexican American populations, despite the fact that the people have repeatedly asked for Chicano bishops to lead them. In 1971, when the See of Brownsville, Texas, was open (and the area is nearly 90 percent Chicano!), *Raza* organizations urged the hierarchy to choose a Chicano and named possible candidates. Instead an Irish American was chosen.

Most tragic of all, the Church continues to deal with Chicanos on a largely superstitious basis, lulling them into being passive, accepting believers who never question. The Cursillo movement has given a needed shot in the arm to Mexican American Catholicism, but unfortunately the proportion of bishops and priests who have been exposed to Cursillos or are even aware of the Cursillo principles of co-responsibility and priest–lay people cooperation, is minuscule. This is one reason why priests are so far out of touch with their Mexican American parishioners.

Non-Spanish speaking American priests (mostly Irish-American) continue to dominate the organized religious life and worship of Chicano Catholics. The sermons I hear them preach in church today have not changed one word from those I heard as a boy growing up in Los Angeles. They still exclusively dwell on the three aspects of the "ideal" Christian life: creed, code, and cult. Proper individual moral behavior (code) and not social justice is repeatedly emphasized from pulpit and confessional. Steady Mass attendance (cult) is inculcated as a primary religious value, even prior to service of those in need. And one's formal, articulated knowledge of the catechism (creed) is held up as a means to sainthood, instead of urging that people become action-oriented in the selfless service of their own people and others less fortunate.

Never once have I heard a priest tell the people from the pulpit (in churches where the majority of the people are Chicanos) to be proud of who they are. Never have I heard a sermon on the Mexican's civil and human rights, and how to win them. To my knowledge no bishop or priest in Los Angeles has ever spoken in church on the Church's own social principles of equal distribution of wealth and the workingman's right to organize and fight for a just wage. There is no question that the code, cult, and creed are important in the life of organized religion; but unless man's social duties and rights are also taught and actively fostered, the Christian "ideals" become only another means to selfishness, not salvation.

The recently formed Chicano priests' organization, PADRES (acronym for Priests for Religious, Educational, and Social Rights) has suggested a radical and exciting idea, which for a time had the Irish American Church leadership scared stiff. They suggested the formation of a Chicano Catholic Church, a national church within the Roman Catholic Church but not under the control of the U.S. hierarchy. It would be accountable only to the Pope.

Such a national church would enable Chicano lay people and priests to assume more responsibility for meeting their own religious needs as well as for taking an active, decisive role in determining precisely what those needs may be at a given time. We would be able to create our own unique liturgy. Presently, the Mariachi Mass is popular, but it is only a stop-gap measure, using Mexican rhythms to cover up the obvious inadequacies of the Roman rite. And we would be able to develop our own theology—a theology of *la raza!*

But the idea of a Chicano Catholic Church remains only an idea. That's why top Church leaders dismiss it now as an idle threat of separatism. And many of the Chicano priests who were the founding fathers of PADRES and who most vigorously promoted the idea of a separate church have since left the active priesthood. This lets the hierarchy off the hook in one sense, but in another, it spells potential disaster when priests are saying the Church isn't even worth fighting about anymore. Apparently many of these men did not think they had a fighting chance because of the recurring opposition from Church superiors and mounting frustration of having good ideas which the Church opposes and won't allow to be implemented.

The only answer may be a complete break. "I think it's great when a priest leaves the Church," a friend of mine recently said. "Any priest who don't quit is going no place. I don't care who he is." In my opinion, if all the oppressed priests in the Church (which is almost all of them) were to leave the institutional Church, they would be in a far better position to see what's going wrong as well as be in a strong enough bargaining position to return to organized religion like decision-making men and not like the powerless subjects and subordinates they are now.

If priests and lay people ever start acting on ideas like that, or the hundreds of others which have been discussed since the Vatican Council, there will be far-reaching and meaningful changes for Catholics, Chicanos included. Until then, a lot of us Chicanos thank God the *Católicos por la Raza* are still around, angry as hell, and ready to deal with the issues.

II

ON THE TOP FLOOR of one of downtown Los Angeles's tall office buildings is the law office for the local branch of the Mexican American Legal and Education Defense Fund (MALDEF). Any visitor would have a hard time telling the lawyers, who are all Chicanos, apart from the clients, many of whom are *barrio* youths in trouble with the law. About the only indication is that the lawyers sometimes sit on the business side of the desks.

The morning I visited with them, attorneys Miguel Garcia and Percy Duran were dressed informally, in sport shirts and slacks. And Tony Rodriguez, another attorney, who was dressed in a T-shirt, looked very much like the *vato loco* he used to be when he was growing up in the projects in one of East L.A.'s toughest neighborhoods. Besides their informal appearance, the ideas which they shared with me were in many ways typical of the new breed of radical lawyers coming out of today's law schools. But their radical spirit and style is closer to that of Zapata and Che than that of Clarence Darrow or William Kunstler.

They joined MALDEF, a public interest law firm which has been called the legal arm of the Chicano movement, because they wanted to help their people as lawyers. Now, less than a year on the job, they are planning to leave MALDEF to start their own law firm, *Abogados de Aztlan* (Lawyers for Aztlan), a firm that will be distinctively and uniquely Chicano in origin, design, and purpose.

As they explained their plan, the first step will be to form a profit-making law office. But the profits, aside from what is needed to run the office and pay modest salaries, will not go into any one individual's pocketbook. Instead the money will be used to finance still another office, a "People's Law Office" in the *barrio* where legal services will be provided to poor Chicanos at no cost to them. Finally, as profits increase from the money-making office, there will be more capital to invest in economic development within the *barrio* or in support of *La Raza Unida* candidates for political office, et cetera.

"We entered law school with the original intention of going back to the communities we came from, and this is our way of doing it," says Percy Duran. "It's not that I don't like it here at MALDEF but economic and political development are priorities for our people and we can't do those things as part of MALDEF." Duran, Garcia, Rodriguez, and four other Chicano attorneys, who comprise the newly formed *Abogados de Aztlan,* will soon open their new law office in downtown L.A., near the MALDEF office.

A board of directors is currently being formed and will consist of the *Abogados,* Chicano law students, and *barrio* people from the Los Angeles area. "With money comes power to exploit others—to use that money for your own ends," says Miguel Garcia. "And this is why in the concept we're developing, the money won't be any one individual's, it's going to be the collective group (board of directors) that decides where the money goes." The board will decide exactly how much will be allocated for salaries, and how much can be invested in such community projects as food co-ops, communes, businesses, political campaigns for Chicano candidates, et cetera. The idea, then, is to use the money-making skills of the young lawyers to eventually help create a strong economic base within the *barrio*. And besides investing money in the community, the *Abogados* will also direct their energies to serving poor Chicanos in need of legal counsel and defense.

Although MALDEF enables them to take most of the police malpractice and abuse of authority cases involving Chicanos, neither MALDEF nor its rural counterpart, California Rural Legal Assistance (CRLA), is able to engage in economic development and political activities because their sources of funding (Ford Foundation and Office of Economic Opportunity) prohibit such extra-legal activities.

Money to start the new *Abogados de Aztlan* law firm came from a grant awarded by the Catholic Church's Fund for Human Development.

Miguel Garcia, 28, came to the United States when he

was 11 and speaks English in the soft accents of his native Jalisco. "We decided that because there are so few Chicano lawyers," he said, "it would be more important to form a group to primarily provide monies to develop the community economically. If the lives of Chicanos and their role in society are to be changed, it will only be because the power of our people is increased and we are able to bargain with the power." He added that practicing law with groups like MALDEF and CRLA is all right as far as it goes but that the only way to change the present balance of power in favor of Chicanos is through money and jobs in the *barrio*.

Like many Chicanos who have identified closely with their people's struggle for justice and have tried to organize within the community, the *Abogados* have frequently been harassed and prevented from being effective by government agencies and other powerful organizations. In 1971, Garcia and another activist Chicano law student, Ricardo Cruz, took and passed the California Bar Exam, which ordinarily would have entitled them to practice law in the state. Instead, both received letters from the State Committee of Bar Examiners stating that they would not be certified as attorneys pending an investigation into their "moral" character.

Garcia immediately called the Committee and asked for an explanation. A man who identified himself as Harold Woods, administrative secretary for the Committee, told Garcia that he was being help up because of his activities in the Chicano movement. "Woods told me about demonstrations that I didn't even remember, like the time we picketed the City Council demanding more Chicano representation."* After several months of waiting, Garcia (who had never been arrested or convicted of any crime but had only been seen at demonstrations by the Committee's informers) was finally certified. Cruz has not been allowed to practice law, however, because he is still under "investigation."

*The Los Angeles City Council, with fifteen elected seats, is supposed to be representative of the city's 1.1 million Chicanos, yet there are no Chicano council members.

Such harassment and intimidation are intended to keep Chicano law students and lawyers from being active in the movement and to serve as a warning that if they become active, they will not be allowed to practice law in the state. "The Bar Association is afraid," says Garcia, "because they see Chicanos with a new philosophy, and they sense the danger to the structure which has existed for so long. If people don't conduct themselves as they see proper lawyers conducting themselves, maybe we don't have as much respect for the legal system as they think we ought to have. But our primary responsibility is to our people and not the system."

Antonio "Tony" Rodriguez grew up in the *barrio* and speaks with a pronounced Chicano accent, the kind many Anglo schoolteachers so intensely dislike, which may partly account for Tony's defiant, antiauthoritarian attitude. "I've been busted a few more times than either Ricardo or Miguel," he says. "I get picked up fairly often; it's on schedule, every two or three months. The Man's been on me for a long time because I grew up in this city and was active in the community even before I went to law school. I guess it was just luck or something that they didn't hold me up like Miguel and Ricardo."

Tony believes that a People's Law office where the emphasis will be on political and economic development is the most important thing Chicano lawyers can be doing at this time. "I really don't see the law itself as so much of a great help. Especially now, I think we're on a trend where a lot of constitutional liberties and guarantees are going to be curtailed pretty much by the Supreme Court decisions. I don't see the law as making that much of a difference except to make repression look legal, look reasonable, look as if you're being given the right to a fair and speedy trial while you're really being repressed."

Rodriguez believes that the law is at best an imperfect tool to be used on behalf of defenseless people; but it is no real answer to the deep-rooted problems within the *barrio*. One reason for the law's inability to help effect change is that there are not enough committed lawyers who want to work together to bring about meaningful change for the poor. "If I stayed with MALDEF, and I like the work here, I'm really not going to do that much. There's not much I can do. Not much even five hundred lawyers can do or one hundred can do in L.A. County. A concerted effort could do it, but you don't even have four hundred radical lawyers in L.A. County altogether."

Rodriguez says that he has seen many Chicanos excel in this society as lawyers, doctors, or teachers. But they are not really representative of their people because they have the same middle-class ideals and bourgeois aspirations as everyone else. "It doesn't impress me that we now have a few Chicano punks running things instead of *gabacho* punks running things. The people are still being oppressed." "Which only goes to show," adds Miguel Garcia, "that the way to become a non-exploited person in this country is to become one of the exploiters."

Abogados de Aztlan is perhaps the first Chicano professional group that is carefully trying to avoid becoming "one of the exploiters." They don't want to move out of their old communities and away from the people they grew up with. On the contrary, they want to involve themselves even more deeply with their people; fighting alongside them not as social workers or do-gooders but as part of the community.

"Lawyers must begin to fight as part of the people," says Tony Rodriguez. "In the past we enjoyed a certain status. Large incomes. I think I could make $40,000 a year easily. But I think that my idea of what *Abogados* is all about is that we begin to deal with the problems of our people not only as legal minds. We will use our ability to make money to foment economic independence among our people. It can't be any other way. Spending time making money for ourselves is taking us away from our duties as human beings and as revolutionaries. As Che says, the highest form of existence is that of a revolutionary. I imagine that some of the dudes [members of *Abogados*] will leave when we start. . . . It's going to take a lot of dedication."

"How will *Abogados de Aztlan,"* I ask, "contribute to the movement?"

"We're working toward the betterment of ourselves as a people, as a society, and in order to reach that goal we have to sacrifice a lot of our individual and selfish interests," answers Tony Rodriguez. "I want to be a lawyer not so I can make lots of money and buy myself a pad in the hills and a limousine. So then everybody will envy me. I want to be a lawyer in the service of my people. *Abogados* will not merely invest money, but if we really believe in the Chicano movement for self-determination and in the poor people's involvement, we will educate them in the spirit of Aztlan.

"Poor people, and Chicanos are a big part of them in this society, are going to have to see that the capitalist system by definition is one where poor people cannot progress. A system where regardless of whether you or I move on to middle-class ranks, there are always poor people, poor Chicanos, because they're produced as a result of the uneven distribution of resources in this society. We have to educate the people about the evils of capitalism. Really, the never-ending cycle that produces poor people in this society. And what about the exploitation of other people by this society? I don't think that we can pretend to ignore the fact that this society uses seventy-five percent of the fuel combustion of the world. While others freeze or die of heat. Others starve while we eat filet mignon.

"If we look at Cuba," Tony continues, "the revolution had just begun when the war was over because people had to understand that it is possible that people progress as a group, that it is possible for people to move together, and that as progress comes it can be redistributed evenly amongst the people."

Radical lawyer groups, of course, are not new. White lawyers with radical views about serving the poor have organized collectives, sometimes working for only room and board and a few dollars a week. But white lawyers come from a totally different background. In many cases, they are renouncing an affluent life style they have known most of their lives and now repudiate as unsatisfying.

What is unique about *Abogados de Aztlan* is that Chicanos who themselves were once poor or who are the sons and daughters of poor Mexican people in the *barrios* are willing to sacrifice luxuries and comforts they have never known, but which society has urged upon them and which they are now in a position to attain easily.

"Chicano lawyers for the first time," says Tony Rodriguez, "are saying, 'Look, we're going to get our own thing, we're going to run it, and this is for the people, to help organize the people; to help provide money and the type of defense Chicanos need.'"

Chicanos who made good in American society have not "assimilated" but have stayed within their people, willing to invest their earnings and, most of all, themselves in the Chicano movement for economic, political, and social equality.

III

I'M RICARDO. FLY ME TO FREEDOM!

—sign at Chicano rally

THE NEWS MEDIA informed the nation on April 13, 1972, that another plane had been hijacked, a Frontier Airlines 737 Jet from Albuquerque, New Mexico. The hijacker ordered the plane flown to Los Angeles.

When the plane touched down at Los Angeles International, the hijacker did not demand a large sum of money or free passage to Mexico or Cuba, as had been expected. His only demand was for immediate press, radio, and television coverage. He had something important to say to the world.

After being assured that the newsmen and camera crews were on their way, as he had demanded, the hijacker released the twenty-seven passengers and three stewardesses but held the captain and crew at gunpoint in the cockpit of the plane. From the plane a live radio hook-up was quickly assembled and the bizarre press conference was then held.

Earlier that day, rumors circulated in the *barrios* that a Black Beret (a member of a militant Chicano youth organization in New Mexico) had commandeered the plane to demand the release of Chicanos being held as political prisoners. But as the hijacker himself began speaking to the people (he spoke entirely in Spanish) over the live radio broadcast, it became evident that the Chicano inside the plane was a 36-year-old unemployed restaurant worker from East L.A. named Ricardo Chavez-Ortiz.

He had no previous arrest record and belonged to no militant organizations. His act was a spontaneous response to the indignities his family and other poor Mexican people were suffering. His family lived in East L.A. and he had lived there with them until, six months earlier, he had lost his job and gone to Albuquerque to work in a restaurant. The job didn't last long and, unable to find work, he and his family were forced to live off welfare.

His recurrent theme throughout the broadcast was that the "children," "younger generation," and "my family" must be saved from the rampant poverty, discrimination, and economic and social oppression in this country. While his criticisms of "Anglo society" were on behalf of all poor people, his most poignant remarks concerned this society's destruction of the dignity and self-respect of the Mexican people. And throughout his rambling discourse, he warned Anglos to take sober thought about what they were doing to the poor and called upon Chicanos to start working for the betterment of their own people because they "cannot endure any more . . . cannot tolerate more."

At the end of his remarks, he proved what he had said several times before, that he had "no criminal intentions," by pulling the magazine from the .22 caliber pistol. It was empty. Then he pulled a second empty magazine from his pocket and handed the weapon to the pilot.

The following discourse, in English translation,* is essentially what millions of Mexican people heard broadcast live from the cockpit of the plane on that warm Thursday afternoon in April when Ricardo Chavez-Ortiz captured not only a Jet plane and its crew members but the absolute attention of Mexican Americans everywhere as they listened to him voice thoughts and feelings which were also their own:

Good afternoon. This is your friend Ricardo Chavez-Ortiz.

I find myself obligated to, I don't know how to say it, cause this disturbance; ah, I don't know how to tell you it has been an obligation of mine. Up to the present time, I have not been able to satisfy my family with the necessities. Let us say a home that they deserve, that they have clean beds and something good to eat. . . .

I have not been able to obtain these things that they need because I am denied work, be it from discrimination or jealousy or whatever reason.

I have felt an obligation to do this bad deed but not only for the situation of my family but the thing is that it is much more delicate and dangerous for the new generation than you can imagine. You can see things are all screwed up. Nevertheless you don't stop to think about what it is we can do. All you do is let the days go by and maybe tomorrow, maybe the next day, there'll be a chance there will be a new governor or a new President, yakkity, yakkity. . . .

. . . I have a very worthy family and I am going to tell you that in the situation in which we are living we have one couch, or in other words a sofa. Do you know where this sofa came from? My children found it in someone's garbage and brought it home to me. That is what we use. Our beds are beds that were given to us by some good

*The tape from the live broadcast as well as two other taped interviews with newsmen on the plane (but which were not broadcast) were at once confiscated by the FBI. I managed to obtain the FBI translations (the only written evidence available at this writing) and have reproduced them here with editorial changes. The actual live remarks form the substance of what follows. The translation by Special Agent E. Rhead Richards, Jr., is, as far as I can determine, fairly accurate.

people and they are old beds, however, they are very much appreciated; and our ice box that God knows how long ago it was made but that is what we are using. You are welcome to come and see my home to see if I am telling the truth. These conditions are not because I have wasted my money but it is because we have had to use all the money that I have earned.

. . . as you know, on whatever street you go in Los Angeles, the only beautiful people are the people with white skin. They are the well-dressed ones, and the Mexican race is distinguished in all areas, and it is something that is very painful to me. . . .

And so, finally what I wanted was, after having made this flight, I wanted to attract the attention of everyone in the nation and say to everyone once and for all, what type of human beings we are. The destruction amongst our children is fantastic. The children that I have, go and ask them yourselves, they have attended school for many years and they know absolutely nothing. And so, this act that I have just committed I did it knowing that I would probably die because of it and that I would probably go to hell. However, my life does not have as much worth as the lives of so many children. However, the thing is very simple, we do not ask for anything for free. This land we are walking on is Mexican land and so, for this simple reason, we do not come to beg for anything or that anything be given to us or anything else.

I want to tell you that I did not have criminal intentions nor do I have them at the present time. It is something I had to do in order to obtain something for my children. They are in great danger. The thing about them, one of my sons in school where he was obligated to join a gang in which there had been some deaths and one of the teachers called my wife and very cynically told her that not even the police can intervene in this matter. Said the only thing you can do is change him to another school. And so my wife, crying, took him to another school and upon seeing all that she suffered I said to myself, "What kind of man am I that I can't even protect my family!" So then about the third day my son came home saying that at the new school there were also three gangs and he said, "I am not going to school anymore. Why continue going to school when they don't teach me anything?" . . .

This land is Mexican land. . . . The conquerors horde it all based on massacres and bad tricks. Certainly this that I am doing is criminal. It is against the law of these persons, these conquerors, because I don't have the right to arrive at a hospital and be attended to as a human being. So I don't have that right. Of course I don't have the right, I am a Mexican. So that it results that we have to live with what they please to hand us.

We have not asked for one damn penny from anyone. I am proud to say that I take care of my own self and I have asked no one to help me. What I say is that if we come to this land which is ours, in this land we must find where we can sell our labor; where they will pay us what is rightfully ours. We respect the laws, we pay our taxes, and we are not going to burn stores or assault people everywhere. We don't live in this way.

We are Mexicans; we live with the cockroaches and in the most unworthy conditions one could have in this land. . . . The Americans go and send rockets to the moon. Yes, go ahead and do whatever you want to do while we become rebellious. . . . Because now we can't endure any more. We cannot tolerate more; we cannot endure more.

I am a man who is right now thirty-six years old and I don't have any matters pending with the law. I don't have any matters pending with anyone. If I owe money in any place, it is because my work was taken away from me or something happened but it was not because I did not have intentions to pay . . . because you all know the salaries we have the right to obtain. These salaries are not enough to pay the rent. . . .

. . . In time past I was working at [a] restaurant. . . . This job was taken away from me because of jealousy, and the boss said, "You are a good person but I am not able to leave you in this job." Then I did not have anything to offer my family, I was several days behind in my bills and cynically I was told that I did not have the right to obtain help or money to provide for my family what they needed. But before this, I realized that one of the boys from there, you know how the Mexicans are . . . you tell them to do it and they do whatever you want them to do because they are good people. Then these boys where they lived went and paid their rent and the landlord said, "Look boys, go on back to your apartment and I'll bring you the receipts later."

And the boys, believing everything anyone tells them, they waited for their receipts. Now if you don't believe me, go and ask them. The landlord, that son of a bitch, came back with the receipts and forced them to pay the rent again. Yes, sirs, that is how things are.

If that is what the laws are like, then the laws are for the protection of the capitalists or, in other words, to protect the government. And for us, well . . . let's wait and see what happens. What I need to say to you and that you need to pay very close attention to . . . on the path we are following, there are going to come some very disastrous and terrible days. In these days the Mexican people are not going to tolerate more. They are not going to endure any more. Why wait until this day arrives? Why don't all of you leave your work and your homes? We want the justice that we rightfully deserve. Don't be cowards; I for myself don't ask anything. . . . They can send me straight to hell. But these children are the ones that have a world ahead of them; a world that can be one of happiness, and why not, gentlemen? Certainly this should be so. This land that we are working on was a divine gift. A gift that God gave and did not distinguish between people. He put it here so that all of us could live and be happy. Nor would He ask us that we make sacrifices to Him. He ask only that we love Him.

[It appears that at this point there was an interruption in the communication from the airplane. Apparently he was still broadcasting but it was not being picked up by the station.]

So gentlemen, please forgive the interruption. This has been the moment when all of you should go and ask justice for your children. Don't be egotist or [unintelligible]. These children are also sons and daughters of God. Don't always just think about your good clothes and having enough to eat and your good friends. Think about these children; think about the injustice that is being done to them. Think about all this; this great injustice that is being done to them. This is not right. It is not right because a world, a world which is built with great effort, and the person that leads it fails, this person is a criminal.

These wars [Vietnam War] that have been fought have been a crime. They have been a crime because these people have gone to join and fight with others and for what reason? For myself, if someone I have to fight and kill, let it be for maintaining justice for my home or for my children or for their future. But just to go and steal, I don't agree with this. I don't agree with this and if I've ever been a thief, you can kill me. Then I would like before anything happens to me, and I am sure something will happen, I would like to hear that the people join together and ask in a very definite way for justice.

There is Mrs. Bañuelos,* another proud product of the society of which we are talking. She has trampled on a lot of people and because of this, she is a big son of a bitch. This is the same person that was given the right to occupy the position of Treasurer of the Nation. No gentlemen, the government should [be] a dignified and respectable thing. Only very capable people and good-hearted with good intentions who hope for a better future have the right to obtain positions like this. . . .

They say the police have written on their cars "To protect and to serve." To protect and serve whom, only themselves. The police are the only ones who have authority to carry a pistol and the license to kill. Very simply, I have great fear of going out on the street because I am afraid that at any moment a policeman will take out his pistol and shoot me, or someone else might kill me.

I consider [the *gringos*] good businessmen; I consider them heroes, but what I do not go along with is that my children are treated like vile beasts. I would rather die, gentlemen, than to continue living with these horrible conditions. And I am one hundred percent certain that if I should die, even after death, if God is willing, that I will come back after being in the tomb and be at the heads of these son of a bitches who have destroyed the pride and dignity of our race which is the Mexican race. . . .

*Mrs. Ramona Bañuelos (a prominent, wealthy Mexican American businesswoman in L.A.) was nominated by President Richard Nixon and subsequently confirmed by the Senate as Treasurer of the United States. During the Senate investigation into her qualifications, it was discovered she was hiring "illegal aliens" from Mexico. She denied knowledge of the fact that many of her employees were "wetbacks" and vowed to keep closer security check on her workers. In the *barrio* it is common knowledge that she has made her fortune in the Mexican food business exploiting cheap labor from Mexico.

I was held captive* by a woman by the name of Tomasa Ramirez in Otay on the other side of San Diego, and I was kept in captivity for two years and all I had was the right to search through the garbage cans for something to eat. I also worked for two years without being paid one single cent. Where was justice at that time? Where were the authorities? So that . . . well, that's all right. This was part of the American society because I was here illegally.

Now since I have been here legally, I went to work for Mr. [unintelligible], 8635 Wilshire Boulevard. I worked for him eight years, fifteen hours a day, sometimes sixteen or seventeen hours a day, and all I ever received was the right to have one plate of spaghetti to eat and work like a dog, and I can prove it. To make a long story short, I worked for him for eight years; eight years of bad treatment, until I became ill. I began to have stomach ulcers and . . . nervous tension. . . .

It was a great shame for me to have to go, at my age, and ask for a handout from welfare. Because I am a man of courage, every time I received a check from welfare, I wept and my hands trembled because I had not earned it with the sweat of my brow. My family felt exactly the same way. . . . Well, then, I ask myself, "Are you going to let things continue like this?" Right now at this moment while things are hot, do something about it. But do it in an orderly fashion. Don't cause destruction or damage because this would make me look bad. It would cause me pain in my soul if you were to go and cause some disturbance. Ask for what you need and make them realize that we are also children of God. So, then, in your hands is the remedy to this bad situation. All that I want is for my family not to continue suffering this danger that is now taking place. . . .

I want my family to be saved. I want my family to be useful to our neighbors and to society, a clean society, not a filthy traitorous society like the one we are presently living in. You are the people who

*Chavez-Ortiz entered the country illegally when he was fifteen years old and worked for the Ramirez family. He later returned to Mexico and then re-entered the United States as a permanent resident [legally].

are the ones that make the laws and elect the governments. Well, what are you doing, what kind of governments are you electing? What kind of society are you making? . . . And finally I tell you . . . don't let your wives be the ones to wear the pants in the family because you don't have the guts to go and say this is what we want; this is what is coming to us, and if we can't get what we want, let's leave this city. It is better that we die of hunger in the desert but at least with dignity where they don't treat us like we're garbage. . . .

All I want is for Mexicans to know that this is Mexican land and always will be. There does not exist in the whole world a nation that is for sale. I can assure you that this is the case no matter where you go, but I would die right now but I would not admit to any son of a bitch that my nation is for sale or in servitude. . . .

I could very easily force this plane to go to Mexico and I could have demanded three or four million dollars. I could have done this, and I assure you that I would have been able to avoid capture there because I know my country very well. I am a pretty smart person. And I know how to use my intelligence so that I can get along well with my friends and family. But no, I'm man enough and have enough guts to earn my bread with the sweat of my brow and I resent the indignity of having to be helped by anyone. It bothers me to have to accept. Well, you that are doing these things . . . go ahead and keep doing it. Tomorrow or the next day or some day you are going to see the results.

I respect this country; I respect it because when I crossed the border I came across weeping because I said to God, from now on I'll be able to eat three meals a day. . . . Since that time I eat three meals a day sometimes; since that time I have a roof over my head; a car that isn't worth anything. . . . I am a man that says thanks to the United States of North America for the little bit it has given me. But I protest the treatment that our children are receiving and I demand the protection that my family needs. . . .

And now in this moment, I'm going to demonstrate that I did not have any criminal intentions. One moment please, I need the television camera to be turned on me. . . .

Chavez-Ortiz then handed his pistol and the empty clips

to the captain of the plane and quietly submitted to the FBI agents who were waiting outside the plane.

After Chavez-Ortiz's arrest and arraignment, bail was set at $350,000. Later it was reduced to $35,000, partly because of demonstrations indicating the Chicano community's concern for, and support of, Ricardo Chavez-Ortiz. Again rallying to his support, the Chicano community raised the bond through a fund-raising campaign (mostly $1 and $2 donations from individual Chicanos) and volunteer property owners mortgaging their homes. The Chicano community's support for Chavez-Ortiz was broad based and universal.

In July 1972, Chavez-Ortiz was brought to trial in U.S. District Court to be tried on one count of air piracy. He pleaded not guilty and because of the federal statute (Air Piracy Act) provisions, had in effect only one tenable defense —that of "diminished capacity" or not being "mentally competent and criminally responsible" at the time of the act.

Chicanos resented the implications of the defense, even though it was the only legally realistic course to take. "If he was crazy," said one Chicano, "then every Mexican American who ever stood up to complain about his community's problems is crazy too."

In late July, Ricardo Chavez-Ortiz was found guilty as charged by a federal jury and sentenced to life imprisonment.

The verdict will be appealed.* The court ordered Chavez-Ortiz to undergo psychiatric examination for several months. If the verdict is reaffirmed or not drastically reduced after the appeals are taken, I believe that the *barrio* communities will explode in anger and resentment. "The *locos* are ready to burn," one Chicano from East L.A. told me recently. "If Ricardo has to spend one day serving time, the *locos* will get their *quetes* [guns] and look for justice in the streets!"

*The National Defense Committee for Ricardo Chavez-Ortiz, 2671 West Pico Boulevard, Los Angeles, California 90006, is currently preparing petitions to be presented to the President, asking for Chavez-Ortiz's pardon.

While awaiting the jury verdict, I spoke with Chavez-Ortiz in the corridor outside the federal courtroom in Los Angeles, where the trial was conducted. Several hijackings had recently taken place across the country, and I asked him if he felt hijackers should be punished. "Yes," he answered, "but with justice." If justice is to be done in this instance, most Chicanos agree, Chavez-Ortiz would not have to spend a single day in prison.

Anglo society, he said, can easily tolerate and live with injustice; what they cannot tolerate or live with, is disorder. Chavez-Ortiz committed an act of disorder to highlight rank injustices which are the daily lot of Chicanos and poor people everywhere.

If injustice prevails, and Chavez-Ortiz is sent to prison for the rest of his life, more disorder is certain to follow. Only this time, as many have vowed, the guns will be loaded.

Epilogue

CHICANOS ARE BUILDING a new nation, Aztlan, where we and our children can be free. The struggle for liberation, as evident on the preceding pages, has produced several important breakthroughs. We have confronted our oppressors again and again, making unyielding institutions respond to our demands for justice, human decency, and respect. These gains represent only a small beginning. In the days ahead, every Chicano will be needed to commit himself—to respond to the call of his blood—by being part of the Chicano movement.

Aztlan will be our own independent, free nation where we will no longer be the colonized, exploited, and abused people we have been for generations. This nation is not a myth or dream but an imminent reality whose foundations are being laid at this moment.* Chicanos want change not only for their children and the future generation, as Ricardo Chavez-Ortiz has eloquently pleaded, we also want change for ourselves—*now*.

*In August 1972, members of the Brown Berets, a militant Chicano organization with over 90 chapters in the United States, invaded and occupied Santa Catalina Island, off the coast of California. Twenty-six Berets (including one woman) occupied a hill overlooking Avalon Harbor. According to Beret leader David Sanchez, the purpose of the occupation was to protest the illegal American "occupation" of land rightfully belonging to Mexicans. Authorities in Mexico as well as many Chicano groups in the United States claim that

White liberals tell us that we can't expect change overnight because deep-rooted problems which are centuries old can only be solved over the long course of years of patient effort. Work within the system, they tell us, so you can make changes from within. While most of us are committed to the long and painstaking process of making social change, we also want to see important changes made right now, overnight, and we know it can be done. The liberals forget that the Spanish *conquistadores* in 1521 toppled and destroyed the Aztec empire and enslaved our people. That was done in three years, which is overnight! The U.S. Army and the American government of occupation in 1848 overturned our social institutions and economic structures and left us politically impotent. That happened not over the course of fifty or one hundred years; it happened overnight!

Our people obviously do not have the military might or fire power to make changes in the same way that the Spaniards and Anglo Americans did. But we have an even greater weapon available to us. Sheer numbers! We are strong because there are so many of us and because *la union hace la fuerza* (there's power through unity). And we are not alone as we prepare to make changes for ourselves and our families. We are conscious of being part of a bronze continent, an entire continent of similarly oppressed and alienated *raza.* If the Chicano movement continues to develop and our people continue stepping forward to make their demands known, backing them up by physical presence, Aztlan will become a reality overnight.

Mexico never ceded the Channel Islands (which include Santa Catalina) to the United States at the end of the Mexican War. They point out that the Treaty of Guadalupe-Hidalgo makes no mention of the islands when describing the Mexican territory that would be annexed by the United States. The Berets renamed the island *"Aztlan libre"* (Free Aztlan) and stayed for twenty-four days until, surrounded by armed sheriff's deputies, they were forced to return to the mainland. The Berets have vowed to return and are presently preparing for a second invasion. "Next time," says one Beret, "we'll bring the people of the *barrios* with us!"

Some areas where Aztlan is being built:

Economic Development. This is a basic priority. We need more and better jobs, on-the-job training in important skills, adequate salaries, and good working conditions, especially for *Mexicanos* who are not yet citizens and do not speak English. Their vulnerability has made them easily exploitable by unscrupulous employers. Economic control of our communities must also once again reside within the people. What Chicanos are demanding here is not that brown-skinned exploiters replace the white ones that now plague poor people in the *barrios.* We are demanding nothing less than a completely new order, and the advent of a Chicano economics. "They say economics is pure," says Steve Sanora, a Chicano student at California State College, Los Angeles. "Sure, there are certain things about supply and demand, but it becomes Chicano economics when you take into account the social factor. Chicano economics would be supply and demand determined by our social ethic; it's not a monetary profit, it's a social profit we're looking for." That social profit is the equitable distribution of wealth among our people.

Social Equality. The movement has restored ethnic, racial, and cultural pride for millions of us who were brainwashed in Anglo-white schools. Demeaning caricatures of Chicanos as dumb, sinister, lazy, dirty, and so on, have been forced off the advertising market, but the white man's image of us will probably not change until we have won full economic, social, and ethnic-racial equality.

The Woman's Liberation Movement has contributed many good ideas to Chicana women which they have been able to use in educating the Chicano man. Many Chicanos, of course, still have not yet learned that their women are not merely housekeepers, babysitters, and sex-objects but *compañeras* (companions and co-equal partners). This is crucial to the movement because, as one Chicana told me, *"El movimiento sin mujeres no se gana como el movimiento sin hom-*

bres no se gana!" (without women the movement will not succeed just as the movement without men will not succeed). In the revolution of 1910 in Mexico the *Adelitas* (Mexican women soldiers) fought side by side with their men; without them the war would not have been won. Chicanos have to understand that we are fighting a war now and we need our women alongside us. And those Chicanas who must tend their children at home have an equally important role, because they must educate our children as revolutionaries.

"In no way do I consider the Chicano man my enemy," says Amalia Uribe, a 22-year-old Chicana from Coachella who has worked for César Chavez as a strike leader and is now a labor organizer for the *Hermandad General de Trabajadores* in Los Angeles. "We must be a family, all of us together, for the movement. Where there are differences, we have to educate the man. But in no way do I consider him my foe. I believe that he is another victim of the capitalist system, just as I am. There is no separate movement for women's rights just as there is no separate one for the men. There is only one movement and that is for all our *raza*."

Political Representation. "Racism is at the root cause of the Chicano's political nonrepresentation," says Herman Sillas of the California State Advisory Committee to the U.S. Civil Rights Commission. "And this is true on every level of government: municipal, county, state, and federal." This accounts for there being no Chicano mayor for any big city in the Southwest; no state governor; no city councilman in Los Angeles (in proportion to our numbers we should have three out of fifteen), this nation's most populous Chicano city. There are only four Chicano members of the U.S. Congress and only one Chicano in the U.S. Senate. The Man has cheated us out of political power by a variety of means: gerrymandering of our districts; discriminatory language, literacy, and residency requirements; threat of deportations and violence if we became politically active, et cetera.

La Raza Unida Party (LRUP). This third party movement among Chicanos began as opposition to the racist politics of both major political parties. On the local level, especially in the *barrios* and *colonias,* LRUP is an effective political reality. Crystal City, Texas, was the scene of José Angel Gutiérrez's first organizational efforts for LRUP and showed what could be done when Chicanos were organized as a voting bloc; they captured nearly all of the elective offices formerly held by Democrats. In other areas where Chicanos are not a majority, they can still be organized within LRUP as a crucial swing vote, as was done recently in the race for Los Angeles's 48th assemblyman's seat, where LRUP candidate Raul Ruiz ran as an independent and demonstrated to the Democratic Party that without *raza* support they couldn't win elections. The LRUP vote ensured the defeat of the Democratic candidate in an assembly district that had always been hard-core Democratic; a Republican was elected to office for the first time in the history of that district. In this way, we are winning the respect of the Republicans and teaching the Democrats that we no longer can be taken for granted as their hip-pocket vote.

The Church and La Raza. Chicanos have forced the Catholic Church to make a few token changes within the institution, but it continues to misuse its power, money, and political influence (despite denials of being political, any human institution that owns stock in Bank of America, General Motors, et cetera is political!). What is worse, the Church has once again forfeited its moral leadership within our communities by failing to be on the side of the poor in their struggle for self-determination.

I now have no official status or position within the institutional Church, but Chicanos still call on me to celebrate Mass for them, which I am happy to do. Church officials would frown on this, but even the most conservative churchmen recognize the validity of my ordination. Moreover, according to the theology most priests learn, there are sacred functions (like baptisms, marriages, Mass, et cetera) which laymen and "defrocked" priests can and should perform in emergency situations when there are no priests available. Most Chicanos believe that as Catholics they are in an emergency situation, because the Church has ceased ministering to their unique cultural and religious needs. In that sense, Anglo priests who do not understand our people are not "available" even though many imposing churches and rectories have been built within the *barrios*. An underground Church for Chicanos is thus slowly coming into existence. This may be the beginnings of our Chicano Catholic Church.

Education. The most important area for development as we build Aztlan is the schools. As we have seen, the schools have acted as the single most divisive force within our communities by teaching us formally and by example that who and what we are is inferior and inadequate. The schools have prevented us from truly knowing ourselves, our history, our accomplishments.

Colleges and universities have also done a great disservice to our people by deceiving people into thinking their programs for "minority groups" were actually helping *raza* advance within society. These institutions have established "minority admissions programs" not out of love for the poor and oppressed but because the federal government refuses to allocate funds to them unless they at least appear to be doing something for black and brown people. The insidious thing about such programs is that they give our people the impression that because a few token Mexicans and blacks are allowed on campus, *raza* everywhere are somehow getting a break. And it is not so. The only thing such programs accomplish is that now, instead of one half of one percent, Chicanos represent one percent of the collegiate population. Even if this one percent advances 50,000 or 100,000 more of our people into the middle cass, the rest of us (13 or 14 million in the Southwest) remain poor, illiterate, without jobs or social mobility.

The elementary and secondary schools continue to commit intellectual genocide against our children while the colleges and universities deceive our people into believing that progress is being made. Not only do they deceive us, they have co-opted some of the most promising potential leaders by turning many of the students into "tanned Anglos" or "assimilated" Mexican Americans who later move away from the *barrios*. But the Chicano movement on campus has shamed many of them into returning to their people; for *el que niega su raza ni madre tiene* (he who has denied his race has denied his own mother).

Some of our people have started Chicano Freedom Schools to re-educate our children. Even if the public schools yield to the pressure we have been exerting on them and establish bilingual education programs for our children, Chicano Freedom Schools (like Corky Gonzales's Tlaltelolco School in Denver) will be needed to supplement what the public schools are not equipped to do or do only in a distorted, Anglo way. "My children," says one Chicano father of three, "are bombarded with Anglo values for six and seven hours a day. Teachers don't just teach them the ABCs but how to believe in a way of life. I can see it affecting them. I can see the selfishness they've learned that day in school."

Chicano children must be educated as revolutionaries, which means that they must learn to read and write not because—as they are now taught by the public schools—they will then be able to go to college, get a good job, buy an expensive home, and take vacations in Europe. Our children must understand that reading and writing are skills to be learned so that they, in turn, can teach them to other poor Chicanos (fifty percent of them!) and so that together we can all use our intelligence in contributing to our new nation, Aztlan.

We are building Aztlan, and two potent weapons in our arsenal are confrontation and opposition. But the Chicano movement does not solely exist to criticize and condemn. We are creating a new order, a new humanity, first among ourselves and hopefully as an alternative that can be shared with all oppressed peoples. The central values of this new humanism are honesty and *carnalismo.*

The autobiographical sketch which began this book was my attempt at being honest and truthful in recounting my own experiences. Writing them down was painful, but my aim was that out of the pain would come some healing for both myself and others as well. For honesty can be contagious; it enables others to speak with equal honesty and candor. And if we make the effort to know ourselves, accept ourselves, and be ourselves, this is the basis of human cooperation, personal interaction, and community. For we are called to be honest not only with ourselves but with one another; we are called to be honest with the U.S. government and with Anglo society by making our feelings, our needs, our demands known.

The second value, *carnalismo,* is the social dimension and thrust to personal self-awareness and honesty. We seek to know, accept, and be ourselves for the benefit and service of others. *Carnalismo,* roughly translated as fellowship and sharing brotherhood, means that we work alongside our *carnales* and *carnalas* as members of a *familia.*

Chicanos are fortunate enough to have a natural model for *carnalismo* because many of us have come from large families with relatives and *compadres* forming an extended *familia.* And even the *vatos* in the *barrios* who belong to gangs (the first gangs were formed to protect Mexican territory from foreign invaders) know what it is to depend on others not only for survival and protection but for fellowship as well. The movement has channeled many of the self-destructive tendencies of gang members into the struggle for Chicano liberation because *vatos* could easily comprehend and accept the *carnalismo* concept as applied to all of our people.

We are called to be fully human, fully Chicano, which means that each of us must put his *familia,* his *barrio,* his *raza* before himself. The best interests of *La Raza* come before any individual's comfort, wealth, or position.

Aztlan is being built on the personal sacrifices of Chicanos who say, *"Mi Raza primero!"* (my people come first). They come before my selfish and individual plans or desires.

This nation has always existed in our hearts. And now we are building it with our hands on Mexican soil which has never ceased to be our own.

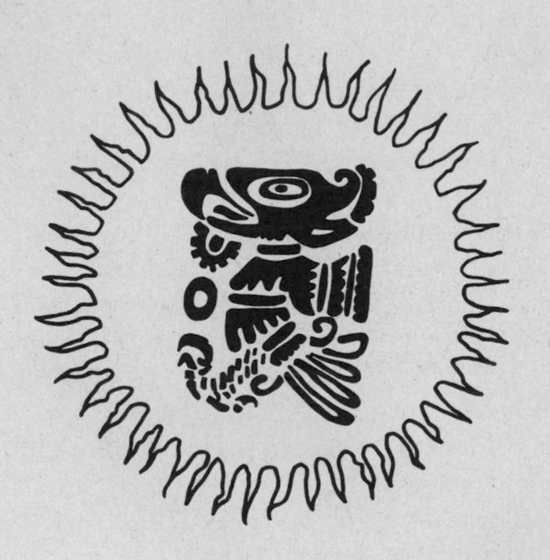

PERMISSIONS

The author gratefully acknowledges permission to quote as follows: to the Russell Sage Foundation for permission to quote from Lyle Saunders, *Cultural Differences and Medical Care* (1954); to Southwestern Cooperative Educational Laboratory for permission to quote from Edward J. Casavantes, *A New Look at the Attributes of the Mexican American* (1969); to Carey McWilliams for permission to quote from his *North from Mexico* (1948); to the Macmillan Company for permission to quote from Grebler, Moore, and Guzman, *The Mexican American People* (copyright © 1970 by The Free Press); to The Viking Press, Inc., for permission to quote from Aubrey Hode, *Martin Buber: An Intimate Portrait* (copyright © 1971 by Aubrey Hode); to The Judson Press for permission to quote from *Educating the Mexican American* (1970) by Henry Sioux Johnson and William J. Hernandez-M.; to Educational Consulting Associates, Menlo Park, California, for permission to quote from Feliciano Rivera, *A Mexican American Source Book* (1970); to Pathfinder Press for permission to quote from *Bert Corona Speaks on La Raza Unida Party and the Illegal Alien Scare* (copyright © 1972 by Pathfinder Press, Inc.); to Dr. Thomas P. Carter for permission to quote from *Mexican Americans in School: A History of Educational Neglect* (New York: College Entrance Examination Board, 1970); to Praeger Publishers for permission to quote from *A Documentary History of the Mexican Americans* (1971), edited by Wayne Moquin and Charles Van Doren; to the University of Chicago Press for permission to quote from Dr. Manuel Gamio, *Mexican Immigration to the United States* (1930); to Harper and Row, Publishers, Inc., for permission to quote from Stan Steiner, *La Raza: The Mexican Americans* (1969); to *Christian Century* magazine for permission to use excerpts from the author's article, "The Killing of Ruben Salazar," January 13, 1971 (copyright © 1971 by the Christian Century Foundation); to *Commonweal* magazine for permission to quote from Celia Heller, "Chicano Is Beautiful" (January 23, 1970); to *America* magazine for permission to use excerpts from the author's article, "Chicanos: Strangers in Their Own Land," June 26, 1971 (copyright © 1971, All Rights Reserved); and to Rodolfo "Corky" Gonzales for permission to quote from "I Am Joaquin" (1967).

Index

The symbol which serves as a tailpiece to the text (on page 196) is the Aztec eagle in the sun, a fitting symbol of Aztlan. Aztlan is the nation which the Aztecs founded and is the spiritual and territorial heritage of today's Chicanos.

Quetzalcoatl, the "plumed serpent" of Aztec mythology, was often depicted as an eagle. Hence the eagle is a reminder of the Aztecs' faith, history, and sacred traditions. It is also a challenge because Chicanos must now liberate this land of their fathers in which they have unjustly been treated as strangers and foreigners.

To the Aztecs, the sun was the essence and source of life. And just as the sun has always given life to the Southwest, the Aztecs who originally inhabited the region have also been a life-giving source. Aztecs and their descendants, the Chicanos, pioneered the Southwest and left an indestructible imprint on the region's institutions, heritage, and culture.

And like the sun, Chicanos are still in the Southwest — still very much a source of life, thought, and creative activity.